A Woman's Drink

A Woman's Drink

BOLD RECIPES FOR BOLD WOMEN

Natalka Burian and Scott Schneider

Photographs by Alice Gao
Illustrations by Jordan Awan

Library of Congress Cataloging-in-Publication Data

Names: Burian, Natalka, author. | Schneider, Scott, 1986- author. | Gao,
    Alice, photographer. | Awan, Jordan, 1984- illustrator.
Title: A woman's drink / by Natalka Burian and Scott Schneider ; photographs
    by Alice Gao ; illustrations by Jordan Awan.
Description: San Francisco : Chronicle Books, [2018] | Includes index.
Identifiers: LCCN 2018004035 | ISBN 9781452173290 (hardcover : alk. paper)
Subjects: LCSH: Cocktails. | Alcoholic beverages. | LCGFT: Cookbooks.
Classification: LCC TX951 .B84 2018 | DDC 641.87/4--dc23 LC record available at
https://lccn.loc.gov/2018004035

Manufactured in China

Design by Vanessa Dina
Typeset by Frank Brayton

10 9 8 7 6 5 4 3 2

Chronicle books and gifts are available at special quantity discounts to
corporations, professional associations, literacy programs, and other
organizations. For details and discount information, please contact our
corporate/premiums department at corporatesales@chroniclebooks.com
or at 1-800-759-0190.

Chronicle Books LLC
680 Second Street
San Francisco, California 94107
www.chroniclebooks.com

For all of our friends, family, colleagues, and guests
who have supported Elsa and Ramona over the years

CHAPTER 6

DRINKING TO GET SEXY 114

Setting the Mood AKA Rose Petals on the
Bed and in Your Glass: **Rose Tequila Sleeper** 116

Best Drink for Making Up:
Cucumber, Mint, and Absinthe Julep 118

When Staying in Is Better than Going Out:
Rosemary and Apple Rye Sour 121

The Drink to Make for a One-Night Stand:
Tequila and Habanero Sour 122

Your Favorites' Favorite: **Aviation** 124

CHAPTER 7

DRINKING IN THE MORNING 128

Make a Mimosa You Didn't Even Know Was Possible:
Mimosa with a Twist 130

Shock and Surprise—Turn a Sunday Morning Favorite Green:
Tomatillo Bloody Mary 132

When You Take Brunch Seriously: **Elderflower Bellinis** 135

Monday Is Coming, so Make the Most of It:
Death in the Afternoon 138

Your Favorites' Favorite: **Cosmopolitan** 141

CHAPTER 8

DRINKING WITH PEOPLE
WHO DON'T DRINK 142

What to Make for Your Pregnant Friend When
She Doesn't Want People to Know She's Pregnant:
Basil, Pomegranate, and Bay Leaf Soda 144

Just Not Drinking? That's Cool:
Jalapeño Blackberry Lemonade 146

Some of the best times with friends

and family begin with cocktails. Unfortunately, many people believe that craft cocktails are formal, inflexible, and nearly always the domain of men. The pre-Prohibition-cocktail craze has produced bars, books, articles, and nostalgia for a time when women couldn't vote or go out alone. The spirit of women in these spaces is demure, and accompanied. This often meticulously copied historical cocktail culture is wildly limiting. Mixing and sharing drinks should be an adaptable, informal, and joyful practice, and not a masculine pastime by default.

When my husband, Jay Schneider, and I opened Elsa in 2008, there were a number of excellent cocktail bars flourishing in New York City. Milk and Honey was the first of its kind, heralding the return of classic cocktails and craft originals, and from there, classic-cocktail dens grew exponentially. Most of these watering holes shared much in common—lengthy and intimidating drink menus, rules of conduct, and an old-fashioned sense of propriety. In this wave of cocktail bars, it was common to see mustachioed bartenders begrudgingly serving perfectly mixed drinks in dark, leather-covered interiors.

I was stunned by the overtly masculine decor and vibe at these places, and the sometimes joyless tone of the service. Each place was like a variation on the last—the interiors were beautiful man caves, with professional, but sometimes surly, men serving the drinks. But the drinks, they were always great.

We wondered what would happen if we opened a bar where women would want to drink, too. The interior would be unapologetically feminine; the cocktails would still be perfect; the music, fun; the atmosphere, lively; and the service, knowledgeable, but kind and welcoming. Our goal with Elsa was to make drinking cocktails in New York more accessible and always fun.

Happily, we made that vision a reality on the Lower East Side of Manhattan, and then expanded it to Ramona in Greenpoint, and to a second Elsa in Cobble Hill, two neighborhoods in Brooklyn. I love this line of work because it feels so alive—our businesses are an active part of our communities. Each location provides a place for people to gather to celebrate or plot, a haven to relax, a place to meet the love of your life or the love of your night. We've held countless weddings, birthday celebrations, baby showers, and fund-raisers within our walls, and it really feels like we've experienced those hundreds of milestones with the members of our community.

That sense of community is strongest among our team of talented and ingenious staff. Our ability to grow and provide an always evolving experience to our guests relies on our collective creative power. So much about this journey has been collaborative. None of these projects would have materialized without the visionary talent of our entire team, but especially my brother-in-law, Scott Schneider.

I met Scott on his eighteenth birthday at a bar on Avenue A. He'd come to visit Jay, my boyfriend at the time, the summer before he started his first semester at Pratt. Luckily for us, Scott took a job a couple of years later as a bar back when we first opened the doors of the original Elsa nearly ten years ago, and has never left our family business. Scott now oversees the cocktail program at each of our bars, and has become our business partner.

I'm lucky because I get to work with my friends and family every day, and this book is no different. I believe we are at our best—and are able to offer our guests the best experience—when we work collaboratively, and feel encouraged to try everything one, ten, or fifty different ways until it is the best, and unlike anything else out there.

The goal of this book is the same, to bring you the very best, to bring you something unlike anything else. There won't be any etiquette lessons here. There will be no pontificating about glassware or quality of ice. This book will show you how to make a lot of really great drinks, and empower you to improvise and experiment with each recipe. Forget those books and articles that perpetuate the false idea that innate skill, or tons of practice, or loads of special equipment are essential for showing your friends and family a good time. The truth is, anyone can make a perfect drink, even if that person knows nothing about artisanal bitters, has limited time, or is living on a budget.

No one should ever feel intimidated mixing, drinking, or even talking about cocktails. We will debunk some of the myths being circulated and encourage you to call anyone out on them, whether it's a mansplaining suspendered bartender or a pompous uncle.

The recipes you'll find here can be made in any kitchen, from your grandma's to the one at the Airbnb you're staying in. Many come with an Elevation Note, so if you're feeling ambitious, or you have access to some bar equipment, you can really go for it and put these drinks over the top. But, if you don't want to avail yourself of those notes, then don't—the drinks you prepare will still be delicious.

I'm excited to bring the fun we have with cocktails at Elsa and Ramona to everyone, but especially to all of the women out there who felt hushed up or left behind in the speakeasy cocktail craze. Everyone should feel confident—even powerful—when it comes to serving, sharing, and inventing new drinks for and with their friends and loved ones.

Some of our recipes require bar tools, and some don't. The list that follows includes everything you'll need to prepare the cocktails in this book. You certainly don't have to go out and buy all of these items. In fact, you probably have many of them already. But if you are planning on investing in tools for your home bar, this list is a good place to start. It includes all of our favorites; each of these tools is reliable and efficient.

Tall glasses, any kind

Many of the recipes found here are served best in a tall glass filled with ice. Any tall glass that holds about 12 oz [360 ml] will do.

Rocks glasses

Most rocks glasses hold 8 or 10 oz [240 or 300 ml]—either works great.

Coupe or champagne flute

We've included a lot of festive recipes that call for sparkling wine, so naturally we want you to be prepared with your preferred glass for pouring the prosecco or champagne.

Wineglasses

Wineglasses are the workhorses of your cabinet. They're not just for vino; they're perfect for our Sangria (see page 81) and Aperol Spritz (page 110). In a pinch, you can use these for almost any cocktail.

Shot glasses
Pretty self-explanatory!

Thermos,
or other subterfuge-friendly container
When taking your entertaining on the go, be stylish and safe.

Plastic cups!
For outdoor drinking, we love the classic clear 12-oz [360-ml] Solo cup, but any plastic cup will do.

Mugs
A 10- to 12-oz [300- to 360-ml] mug will accommodate many of our recipes, including the hot cider (see page 148) and Moscow Mule (page 168).

Punch bowl
Odds are you know somebody with a punch bowl, so there's probably no need to go out and buy one—although many thrift stores have a pretty compelling and reasonably priced punch bowl selection. We have several recipes that can be scaled up and served this way for a party with lots of thirsty guests.

1-L glass swing-top bottle

These are ideal containers for storing or serving mixtures of all kinds, including infusions, shrubs, and even premade cocktails. Their airtight seals make them an invaluable storage vessel. And because they're tall and slender, they don't take up a ton of refrigerator real estate, either.

Pitcher

A good-quality glass pitcher is perfect for mixing and serving. Any pitcher that holds at least 8 cups [2 L] is fine.

Slow cooker

Again, if you don't have one, somebody you know probably does. You can make lots of delicious hot drinks with this one piece of equipment—and when it comes to holiday cocktails, nothing beats a slow cooker for ease of serving. You can make hot drinks on the stove top if you absolutely must, but chances are (especially if it's a holiday), all of your burners are already occupied.

Spoon, ladle, whisk

Keep your mixing and pouring options open! In addition to a ladle and whisk, you'll need an assortment of spoons—bar spoon, wooden spoon, teaspoon—so you're ready to stir things up any time. Odds are you have many of these items in your kitchen already.

Wooden muddler

A muddler is nice to have around for old-fashioneds and many non-alcoholic drinks, but we offer several muddler-free options and work-arounds in our recipes, so don't despair if you don't own one.

Paring knife

For fixing garnishes, make sure you have a nice, sharp paring knife in your silverware drawer or knife block.

Large (8 inch) and small (4 inch) chinois strainers

You'll be doing a lot of straining over the course of your cocktail-mixing life, and a couple of these cone-shaped, very fine mesh strainers are a must: a large (8 in [20 cm]) and a small (4 in [10 cm]). They might seem like superfluous items to have around, but they are incredibly useful in the kitchen. You can employ them in your most complex recipes, like the Rose Tequila Sleeper (page 116), but also use for rinsing fruit or draining a box of pasta.

Juicer

Nearly all of our recipes call for freshly squeezed juice. One of the most reliable, affordable, and space-saving juicers on the market is the Ra Chand manual citrus juicer. In a pinch, you can hand-squeeze citrus, but we promise this investment will make your life a lot easier.

Large mason jars

I make all of my infusions at home in 1-qt [960-ml] mason jars, simply because they are sturdy, and easy to clean and cap. They're also inexpensive, and can accommodate flowers—or anything!—when they aren't being used for infusions.

Straws

Straws are a must-have whenever you mix drinks. When you stick a straw in a glass, you're providing a stirrer, a beverage delivery device, and even a garnish. Make sure you always have straws on hand, whether in your kitchen cabinet, in the trunk of your car, in your picnic basket, or in your suitcase, if you're going on vacation.

Cocktail shaker and Hawthorne strainer

While not every recipe calls for the use of a cocktail shaker, this piece of equipment is important to have around. We recommend a set of two weighted shaking tins, one of which fits into the other. It's called a Boston shaker. The cobbler shakers found in most stylish houseware sections (you know the ones we're talking about—the ones with the screw-top lid and cap) are lovely, but they don't pull their weight behind the bar or at home. You'll also need a Hawthorne strainer—a flat strainer with a spring around its underside, that fits over the shaking tin.

Mixing glass

For all of your stirred drinks, you'll want a glass that's large enough to accommodate ice, the cocktail you're working on, and a spoon. In a pinch, you can use a pint [480-ml] glass, but there are lovely mixing glasses on the market—some made of crystal, some that are spouted. They're all good. Just make sure yours holds at least 2½ cups [600 ml] of liquid.

Popsicle mold (and sticks!)

You can get these pretty much anywhere, just make sure they pop out a 3- to 4-oz [90- to 12-ml] frozen treat. We prefer a silicone mold, which makes extraction a cinch, but if all you have is plastic, that works too.

Jiggers

There are lots of different styles and sizes of jiggers out there. Regardless of style, we recommend a set of three that includes a 1-to 2-oz [30- to 60-ml] jigger, a ¾- to 1½-oz [20- to 45-ml] jigger, and ½- to ¾-oz [15- to 20-ml] jigger.

Funnel set

You'll always be glad to have a funnel around, whether you're decanting an infusion or transferring freshly squeezed juice to a more beautiful container. A set of two, one large and one small, will last you a lifetime.

Atomizer

We don't use atomizers a lot, but when we do, it really elevates a drink in the flavor and aroma departments. It won't be the end of the world if you don't have one, but it's a decadent way to finish a drink with finesse. You can find simple atomizers online and at most well-stocked kitchen stores.

Mandoline

This is another bonus weapon in your bar arsenal. You may already have one of these in your kitchen for regular cooking duty, and if you do, great! This is a tool that painlessly guarantees uniformly thin slices of fruits and vegetables for all kinds of beautiful garnishes.

Etc.

This is your home bar, and it should be a true extension of your home and the things you love. So anything you want to add—a beautiful ice bucket and tongs, a stash of amazing paper umbrellas, or a variety of twisty straws—is up to you. The garnishes we suggest in these recipes are just that: suggestions. Your hosting style should reflect your taste— whether you garnish every drink you serve with a fresh orchid or a Little Debbie snack cake.

If you pick up a few essential skills, you can make almost any cocktail in the world. You'll use some of the basics, like shaking, stirring, and straining, for nearly every recipe in this book. We also help you learn a few more advanced cocktail-making skills, like preparing your own infusions and syrups. With this information in your pocket, you'll be able to make dozens of classic cocktails, but more importantly, you'll be able to experiment and develop your own recipes.

Shaking, Stirring, and Straining

Shaking, stirring, and straining are basically all about water—how much you mix in and how much you take out.

To shake a drink, add 5 to 7 ice cubes (about 1 oz [30 ml] each) to the liquid in either of your shaking tins (I'm assuming you have a Boston cocktail shaker), whichever feels most comfortable. Firmly smack your second tin, bottom-up, inside the first tin, creating a strong seal, so that you can shake confidently without any spills. Shake with both hands—vigorously—for 20 to 30 seconds. Don't worry about form, just be mindful of force.

For single-strained cocktails, separate the tins, and make sure all of the liquid is in the larger one. Place your Hawthorne strainer on top, and holding it in place with your forefinger and thumb, pour out the liquid into the prepared glass. Don't hesitate to push your forefinger down, clamping the front of the strainer more firmly—beyond the rim of the tin—for a cleaner pour.

To double strain, instead of straining directly into a glass, use your other, nonpouring hand, to hold your small chinois strainer over your prepared glass. This additional strainer insures that not a single chip or sliver of ice will be floating in your drink. Double straining is often used for cocktails served up, with no ice, for completely smooth sipping.

When you make a stirred drink, use a mixing glass that holds at least 2½ cups (600 ml). Once all of the ingredients have been added to the glass, fill it entirely with ice. If all of your cubes are uniformly large, crack two or three and put them on top for a quicker, colder, and more even stir. To crack ice, hold the cube in one hand and use a heavy spoon or muddler to break the ice (be careful!). Proper stirring is an acquired skill, so don't feel bad if you can't pull it off on your first try. Place your bar spoon straight down into the glass, and guide the handle in a circular motion around the rim. Stir for 30 seconds, and place your Hawthorne strainer on top before pouring out into your prepared glass.

Garnishes

We love garnishes, and treat them with respect and care. A drink with a beautiful garnish is another way to make someone feel welcome and special. In a way, it's like a mini–flower delivery. Experimentation with garnishes is highly encouraged, but you should know some basics before striking out on your own. We'll walk you through them all, from proper zesting to making more complex compound garnishes.

Citrus Zests

With a paring knife—or in a pinch, a vegetable peeler—slice a 1-by-3-in [2.5-by-7.5-cm] strip of orange, lemon, or grapefruit zest. If you get a little pith, it's not the end of the world, but make sure no pulp clings to your garnish. Holding the garnish over the glass with the peel facing out, quickly pinch the zest three or four times over your drink to express the aromatic citrus oil onto the surface. Rub the peel side around the rim, and then balance the citrus peel on the edge of your glass.

Citrus Wedges

Lemon and lime wedges are the most universal of garnishes. Make sure you're working with a sharp knife. Begin by shaving off the rough blossom and stem ends of the fruit, making your cuts as small as possible. Cut the citrus in half lengthwise, from end to end. Turn one half cut-side up and make a horizontal cut across the middle, cutting through the fruit and the pith, without puncturing the zest. Repeat with the other half of the fruit.

You can usually get three to four wedges from one citrus half. Hold one half on the cutting board, cut-side up, and cut in half lengthwise, through a line of pith. You should have two equal segments. Cut each one in half again, preserving a thin line of pith across the top of each segment. The wedges should look almost like a cartoon slice of fruit. Because you made those horizontal cuts at the beginning, these wedges are ready to perch on the rim of any glass.

Citrus Wheels

Wheels of citrus, other fruits, and vegetables make simple but elegant garnishes—just make sure the slices are uniform. This can be done with your paring knife, but an adjustable mandolin ensures perfect slices every time. Float thin wheels on the surface of your drinks or fan them along the inside of the glass. Or perch a thicker slice on the rim of the glass, after cutting a single notch from the center of the wheel down the rind.

Sugared or Salted Rims

When you want a perfectly sugared or salted rim—or both!—all you need is a shallow saucer. Pour a thin layer of your sugar, salt, or mixture into the saucer. Dampen the rim of your glass by chilling it, or for a more concentrated garnish, hold the glass upside-down and run a citrus wedge around the rim. Then gently press and roll the outside of the rim in the sugar or salt, keeping the inside clean.

Skewers

The best way to combine garnishes is to kebab them on a 4-in [10-cm] looped bamboo skewer. You can slide on any sequence of cut or whole fruit. You can play with ratio, position, composition and more. A skewer holds your complex garnish together, but also provides an elegant reminder of what's in your drink. For example, a blackberry mint lemonade might be garnished with a skewered blackberry with a mint leaf. You could even fold a bit of lemon zest into the mix, making a little citrusy envelope for the mint before skewering it. Then pop the blackberry on last.

Fresh Herbs

Herbs are another garnish go-to. As you take a sip, the fragrance from a verdant stem of herbs ensures that all of your senses are addressed. The most widely used herbal garnish is a spring of mint, because it's beautiful, sturdy, and easy to come by in every season. When preparing a mint garnish, make sure you start with the freshest possible stem. Strip the leaves off the base of the stem, leaving only the top three tiers of leaves. Trim off most of the stem, leaving about 1 in [2.5 cm] below the remaining leaves. Tuck the sprig into your glass, so that a bouquet of clustered leaves emerges from the drink.

To release maximum fragrance for herb garnishes, clap the prepared garnish between your palms to activate its aroma. For rosemary or thyme, clap the sprigs multiple times. Lay the stems across the top of your glass, too, for a simple and attractive garnish.

If you're garnishing a frothy drink, particularly one that's served straight up, you can float a single, perfect leaf—basil, sage, mint, anything light enough—on the surface for a subdued and artful finishing touch.

Bitters

You don't need bitters for every cocktail, but it is that secret ingredient that draws out all of a drink's subtle flavors, while balancing out stronger notes. The bitters market is constantly expanding, and the flavors range from wormwood, to tobacco, to smoked chile. These mixtures are made with a neutral grain spirit and some mixture of spices, citrus peel, herbs, and even tree bark. These are great to experiment with, but you really only need Angostura in your home bar to make a wide variety of perfect drinks.

If you've just opened a brand new bottle of bitters, be sure to use an extra hit or two until the bottle is broken in. A new bottle of bitters is like a new bottle of olive oil. It needs to be emptied a bit before you get that consistent glug situation going. A newly opened bottle of bitters will drip out inconsistently when shaken. Compensate with a few extra hits to make sure you don't shortchange your cocktail.

What We Talk About When We Talk About Infusions (and Syrups)

Infusions and syrups should not inspire fear. Often, they're incredibly easy to prepare—as long as you use ingredients that pair well for maximum flavor. We offer several infusion and syrup recipes, which can serve as templates for your own experiments (that caraway-infused rye in the Elevation Note on page 108 is one of my absolute favorites). You may see decorative infusions on display at restaurants and bars for months or even years, but we recommend infusing for the time specified in the recipe, and then carefully straining to ensure maximum shelf life.

We suggest infusing spirits and syrups in large mason jars, simply because they're easy and seal well. But once your infusion is ready to use, the pro move is to strain and funnel it directly into a glass bottle. A chinois strainer lined with a coffee filter does the best job.

The more comfortable you become preparing infusions of all kinds, the more vessels you will need on hand to store them. Save your empty liquor and miscellaneous 16-oz [480-ml] glass bottles—and don't forget the caps!—for holding your infusions. You can thoroughly clean almost any bottle by filling it with water and soaking it in a sink full of warm water and a few tablespoons of baking soda. Use a dish towel to rub away any remaining glue. Scrub away any stubborn spots with a scouring pad.

Stockpile empty bottles for the holidays, because infusions make great gifts, too!

A NOTE ON
INGREDIENTS

You may encounter a few unfamiliar ingredients in some of these recipes, but don't be alarmed. Almost everything can be found online, or in your local grocery store. Variations in certain ingredients are inevitable—for example, in the spice level of jalapenos—but you should always taste as you go and adjust to your preferences. We like to use organic ingredients whenever possible, but it is by no means a requirement in the preparation of any of these recipes. If you can't find organic ingredients—or, you don't want to spend your money there—just use whatever is easiest for you. This book should decrease your stress, not add to it.

Try Not To Settle
for Less Than Fresh

You may have seen those plastic lemon- and lime-shaped bottles filled with chemically preserved "juice." If you have any of these in your fridge, or even the old beloved standby, Rose's lime, don't get any ideas about using those shortcuts in these drinks.

All of the citrus fruit juice must be freshly squeezed and thoroughly strained. In a closed container, lemon and lime juice will keep in the fridge for up to 3 days, but for many of these single-serving recipes, squeezing a single lemon or lime will do the trick.

There's a bit more leeway when it comes to grapefruit, orange, pine-apple, mango, and cranberry juice. You can buy these, but make sure you select a high-quality brand that is 100 percent juice.

Set yourself up with an array of spirits when you're building your home bar. Below are a few of our favorite options, from amaro to vodka, in multiple price points.

LEVEL 1 $

rye: Old Overholt

bourbon: Four Roses

gin: Gordon's

tequila: Sauza Blanco

mezcal: Vida de San Luis Del Rio

vodka: Luksusowa

rum, white: Angostura White Oak

rum, dark: Goslings

absinthe: Pernod

brandy: Landy VS Cognac

Scotch: Dewar's

BITTERS AND MIXERS

Angostura bitters

Regan's orange bitters

Hella Smoked Chili bitters

Campari

Aperol

Fernet-Branca

vermouth, dry: Noilly Prat

vermouth, sweet: Carpano Antica Formula

triple sec: Combier

Luxardo Maraschino

crème de violette

Pimm's No. 1

Chartreuse: green and yellow

Velvet Falernum

elderflower liqueur: St. Germain

LEVEL 2 $$

rye: Bulleit Rye

bourbon: Bulleit

gin: Fords

tequila: Espolòn

mezcal: Unión

vodka: Tito's

rum, white: Caña Brava

rum, dark: Flor de Caña 7

absinthe: St. George

brandy: Hine VS Cognac

amaro: Nonino

single malt Scotch: Laphroaig 10

LEVEL 3 $$$

rye: Michter's

bourbon: Blanton's

gin: Plymouth

tequila: Fortaleza

mezcal: Del Maguey Santo Domingo Albarradas

vodka: Aylesbury Duck

rum, dark: Ron Zacapa 23

brandy: Busnell Calvados

single malt whiskey: Yamazaki or Hibiki Suntory

LEVEL 3 EXTRAS

Pisco

Bénédictine

Drambuie

Cointreau

We find inspiration everywhere: in the places we travel, the books we read, the music we listen to, and the meals we eat. But, one of the greatest sources of inspiration is our community. We're fortunate to have a wide network of fascinating friends, neighbors, partners, and guests. The excellent and diverse taste of our community shapes the way we create spaces, recipes, and experiences.

It seemed only natural to go to some of the most interesting women in our communities, our favorites, and ask them what they prefer in their glasses. These are women we admire personally and professionally. They are talented artists, activists, authors, and actors. They are smart, funny, and fascinating—basically, these are the women you want to invite to your cocktail party.

Entertaining and hospitality is so much more than the recipes you choose to make, or the flowers you buy, or the space you prepare. Entertaining is about the people you include; hospitality is about making everyone feel welcome and important. We loved the variety in our favorites' answers and the reasons behind their choices. Their responses reinforced something every host should remember; every guest will want, or need, something different. This book should prepare you to entertain anyone, anywhere, any time, or just take inspiration from the community around you and enjoy a good drink in their honor.

CHAPTER 1

DRINKING FOR ONE

Do you live alone? Want to make an easy Michelada (see page 44) to go with your homemade Sunday egg and cheese sandwich? Are you a single mom who put your kid to bed and just need a drink for God's sake? Here are some perfect drinks for one.

ROUGH DAY AT WORK:
JUST AN OLD-FASHIONED

Here are two spins on an old classic (and one of my all-time favorites). The first version is made the traditional way, with Angostura bitters, a Demerara sugar cube, and a muddler. Don't have bitters or bar equipment? The second version is just as good.

VERSION I:
TRADITIONAL OLD-FASHIONED

1 ROUGH-CUT DEMERARA SUGAR CUBE

2 DASHES ANGOSTURA BITTERS

1½ TSP SODA WATER

2 OZ [60 ML] RYE OR BOURBON

2 TO 3 ICE CUBES, PLUS MORE (OPTIONAL) AS NEEDED

1 LEMON

1 ORANGE

Serves 1

Put the sugar cube in your rocks glass. Add the Angostura bitters and soda water. Muddle until the sugar is dissolved. Pour in your preferred spirit. Add the ice and stir for about 30 seconds. If you like, throw in some more ice.

To garnish the drink, using a paring knife or vegetable peeler, if that's more comfortable for you, peel one strip of zest each from the lemon and orange. With the peel facing out, zest your drink with the strips, one at a time (see page 22). You'll know you've done it right if you can see the citrus oil drifting on the surface. Drop the peels in the glass, creating a citrusy X against the side.

VERSION II:
IMPROVISED OLD-FASHIONED

SMALL PINCH OF GROUND NUTMEG

PINCH OF GROUND CINNAMON

2 TSP ORGANIC CANE SUGAR (OR 2 "RAW SUGAR" PACKETS)

2 OZ [60 ML] RYE OR BOURBON

2 TO 3 ICE CUBES, PLUS MORE (OPTIONAL) AS NEEDED

GARNISHES (OPTIONAL)

1 STRIP LEMON OR ORANGE ZEST (SEE PAGE 22)

1 SMALL SPLASH ORANGE JUICE

Serves 1

Combine the nutmeg, cinnamon, and sugar in your rocks glass. Add a splash of warm tap water, and swirl until the sugar and spices have dissolved. Add the whiskey and the ice cubes. Stir for about 30 seconds and add more ice, if you wish.

If you'd like to garnish your drink by zesting it, go for it! If not, add the orange juice for an extra hit of citrus. Or you can just run the orange around the rim of the glass. You don't need to peel it or anything.

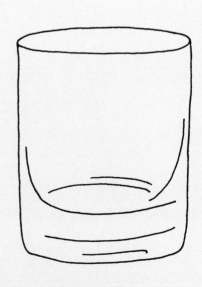

TV NIGHT FOR ONE:
MEZCAL GIMLET WITH APEROL

ICE CUBES

2 OZ [60 ML] MEZCAL

¾ OZ [20 ML] AGAVE NECTAR

1½ TSP APEROL

¾ OZ [20 ML] FRESHLY SQUEEZED LIME JUICE

5 TO 7 ICE CUBES

1 STRIP GRAPEFRUIT ZEST (OPTIONAL; SEE PAGE 22)

Serves 1

This drink is a great nightcap to enjoy solo, because the smokiness of the mezcal mixed with the rich agave evokes a sublime coziness. It's pretty much the embodiment of comfort, so grab a blanket, put on your slippers, and luxuriate. Just make sure you're in close proximity to your remote; this cocktail pairs perfectly with all sorts of binge watching.

Fill a rocks glass with ice. Combine the mezcal, agave, Aperol, and lime juice in your shaking tin. Throw in 5 to 7 ice cubes and shake for about 30 seconds. Strain into your rocks glass. A nice strip of grapefruit zest, squeezed over the drink, makes a lovely garnish, but honestly, it's totally optional. The drink is amazing all on its own.

DRINKS ON A PLANE:
IN-FLIGHT DIY MICHELADA

ICE CUBES

1 OZ [30 ML] MR. AND MRS. T PEPPER BLOODY MARY MIX OR TOMATO JUICE

1 LIME WEDGE

1 TO 2 DASHES HOT SAUCE (ABOUT ½ PACKET), PLUS MORE AS NEEDED

ONE 12-OZ [360-ML] CAN MEXICAN BEER OR LIGHT LAGER

PINCH OF SALT AND PEPPER (OPTIONAL)

Serves 1

You make all kinds of compromises for travel, but you won't have to settle for boring beverage-cart options any longer. This drink relaxes nervous flyers, but it's also light enough that you'll be able to identify the correct luggage at baggage claim. It requires a little planning ahead, so grab that mini–tabasco bottle from your room-service tray, or pick up a packet of hot sauce in the airport food court before you board. For the bloody Mary mix or tomato juice (whatever is available on the flight), use about a quarter of a mini can.

Fill your plastic cup with ice cubes. Pour the bloody Mary mix into your prepared cup. Squeeze the lime into the mix, and throw in that hot sauce.

Slowly pour in the beer, stir to mix all of the ingredients, and taste. Add a little salt, pepper, or more hot sauce so that your drink is to your liking, and enjoy that in-flight entertainment.

FOR THE BREASTFEEDING WOMAN:
PIMM'S CUP WHITE WINE SPRITZER

6 CUCUMBER SLICES

4 OZ [120 ML] DRY WHITE WINE

½ OZ [15 ML] PIMM'S

5 TO 6 ICE CUBES, DEPENDING ON THE SIZE OF YOUR GLASS

3 OZ [90 ML] GINGER ALE

Serves 1

I've had the miraculous and harrowing experience of breastfeeding two babies, and frankly, I have never needed a drink more than during those periods of my life. There are limits to how much you should drink while nursing, but this lower alcohol option allows you to put your baby down for bed, and enjoy a cocktail, while remaining vigilant for any cries in the night.

This drink is also new-parent friendly, because it's incredibly easy to make. You can literally be half asleep and build it right in your glass.

Line your wineglass with cucumber slices, as carefully or sloppily as you like. Pour in the white wine and Pimm's. Add the ice cubes, and top with the ginger ale. Enjoy, and then try to get some sleep.

THE THREE-INGREDIENT MYTH

A lot of cocktail experts will talk about the "golden ratio," the three ingredients that make up any good drink: the spirit, something sweet, and something sour. While this encourages balance—always a good thing—it's also quite a limiting formula. A host of interesting flavor profiles are potentially excluded, like spicy, smoky, and savory.

A better way to mix up your own invention is to start with what you love. Is there a favorite fruit of yours in season? Did you have a meal with an interesting combination of ingredients that you liked? Start with these elements, and work out from there. Balance can all be sorted out later—it's the personality of the drink that should come first.

Deceptively strong
and unapologetically bitter,
just like my soul.

LAUREN DUCA, JOURNALIST

NEGRONI

5 TO 7 ICE CUBES, PLUS EXTRA (OPTIONAL) FOR THE GLASS

1 OZ [30 ML] BARREL-AGED GIN

1 OZ [30 ML] SWEET VERMOUTH

1 OZ [30 ML] CAMPARI

1 STRIP ORANGE ZEST (SEE PAGE 22)

Serves 1

We love this classic as much as Lauren does, and we serve a barrel-aged version of it at all of our locations. While barrel-aging is complicated and generally not practical for home use, we've found a way to cheat this monthlong process by using any high quality, barrel-aged gin. For the sweet vermouth, we like Carpano Antica Formula best.

Add 5 to 7 cubes of ice to a mixing glass. Pour in the gin, vermouth, and Campari, and get your bar spoon. Stir until it's nice and cold, then strain into a rocks glass or a coupe glass. Really, this one can be served up or over ice—it's entirely up to you or your guest. But whatever you do, don't forget to zest and garnish with that strip of orange peel.

CHAPTER 2

DRINKING WITH A PLUS ONE

If an old friend is coming over, or you're sitting around with your roommate, or you're hanging out with a work acquaintance you'd like to know better, here are some recipes to make things more interesting.

ONE GRAPEFRUIT, TWO WAYS:
GRAPEFRUIT GIN AND TONIC AND BASIL PALOMA

1 GRAPEFRUIT

2 TO 4 OZ [60 TO 120 ML]
GIN OR TEQUILA

ICE CUBES

8 TO 12 OZ [240 TO 360 ML]
TONIC WATER OR GINGER
ALE, DEPENDING ON YOUR
GLASS SIZE

4 BASIL LEAVES

2 DASHES HOT SAUCE
(OPTIONAL)

2 STRAWS

Serves 2

Have a friend coming over who loves tequila, but you prefer gin?
Buy a single grapefruit and you're both covered!

Take out two tall glasses. Peel two good strips of zest from the grapefruit
for garnishing purposes (see page 22). Cut the grapefruit in half along
its equator, and squeeze each half into a glass. Give each glass 1 to 2 oz
[30 to 60 ml] of your preferred spirit, depending on your mood and
where you're headed. Add ice cubes to both glasses.

Top the gin with tonic, and the tequila with ginger ale, about 4 to 6 oz
[120 to 180 ml] per glass. Zest the glasses with a strip of grapefruit peel,
pop it into the glass, and add a straw.

Your last garnish will be a couple of verdant basil leaves. Clap each leaf, one at a time, between your palms (as if you were actually applauding) to release the oils and fragrance. Prop two leaves in an abbreviated fan shape against the side of each glass.

ELEVATION NOTE: If you like, add a dash of your favorite hot sauce to your tequila drink to spice things up. If you're feeling adventurous, you can add a dash of hot sauce to the gin cocktail, too!

IMPRESS ANYONE (EVEN SOMEBODY WHO KNOWS YOU VERY WELL) WITH THIS STUNNER OF A DRINK:
DARK AND STORMY

ONE ½- TO 1-IN [12-MM TO 2.5-CM] PIECE FRESH GINGER, PEELED AND MINCED

2 TSP ORGANIC CANE SUGAR

ICE CUBES

2 LIMES

6 OZ [180 ML] GINGER ALE

4 OZ [120 ML] DARK RUM

Serves 2

This is a longtime customer favorite, which dates back to the original Elsa. There are only a few ingredients; the secret to making it special is fresh ginger. For the rum, we like to use Goslings.

Divide the ginger between two tall glasses. Add 1 tsp of sugar to each glass and use a muddler or a dinner fork to mix the ginger and sugar in the bottom of the glass, macerating the ginger. Fill the glasses completely with ice—a full glass of ice is the key to floating a spirit.

Cut each lime in half along the equator and squeeze the juice of one half into each glass. Add 3 oz [90 ml] of ginger ale to each glass, or until they are about four-fifths full. Very slowly and carefully, pour the rum over the ice so that it floats on top of the ginger mixture, creating a visually stunning, classic Dark and Stormy, with a two-tone effect.

Cut two wheels from the remaining lime halves (see page 23). Cut a notch from the center of each wheel through the rind, and perch on the edge of a glass. Add a straw and it's ready to present. Don't forget to mix the layers with the straw—creating a storm in your glass—before you drink.

ELEVATION NOTE: You can add to or replace the ginger with anything you like— strawberries, basil, mint—and create a whole new classic cocktail of your own. Muddle the fruit or herbs of your choice before adding any ice or spirit.

TRANSFORM A CLASSIC COCKTAIL BY SWAPPING SPIRITS: TEQUILA OLD-FASHIONED

½ OZ [15 ML] AGAVE NECTAR

4 DASHES ORANGE BITTERS

4 OZ [120 ML] REPOSADO TEQUILA

ICE CUBES

2 STRIPS ORANGE ZEST (SEE PAGE 22)

2 STRIPS GRAPEFRUIT ZEST (SEE PAGE 22)

Serves 2

If you prefer tequila to whiskey, then whip up a couple of tequila old-fashioneds before a night out. A tequila old-fashioned is a great way to put a bottle of high-quality tequila to good use. Any great reposado will do, but we recommend Fortaleza because it's a fantastic product at a good value. (*Reposado* just means "aged," in this case, in oak barrels, which makes the tequila just as smooth and complex as you'd expect.)

Take out two rocks glasses, and split the agave between them. Add 2 dashes of orange bitters to each. Pour half the tequila into each glass. Throw in a couple of ice cubes and stir briskly until you can feel that the outside of the glass is cold. Add another ice cube or two, and get ready to garnish: Make an *X* with 1 strip of orange zest and 1 strip of grapefruit and sink it into the drink, making sure that the peels are at nose level (and not totally submerged in the liquid) when you take a sip. Repeat with the remaining strips of zest and the second drink.

CONTINUED

ELEVATION NOTE: For a spicier, smokier tequila old-fashioned, substitute Ancho Reyes chile liqueur for the agave, and swap out the orange bitters for smoked chile bitters. Use only 1 dash of the chile bitters in each glass instead of 2.

WHY DIRTY ROLLING SHOULDN'T BE A DIRTY SECRET

Dirty rolling is shaking a drink and pouring out everything from your tin—ice, fruit, herbs, citrus—directly into your serving vessel. It gets a bad rap mostly because it's considered a rough preparation without the finesse and sophistication of straining.

However, if your drink is made with beautiful, fresh produce, dirty rolling can be one way to show off the quality of your ingredients. Because there's no straining it makes a quick and easy, visually stunning presentation.

I go for a Dirty Plymouth
Gin Martini up or
on the rocks, depending
on my mood. Smooth.
Savory. And straight
to the point.

ELEANORE PIENTA, ACTOR

DIRTY GIN MARTINI

2½ OZ [80 ML] GIN

½ OZ [15 ML] OLIVE BRINE

½ OZ [15 ML] DRY VERMOUTH

5 TO 7 ICE CUBES

OLIVES FOR GARNISH

Serves 1

Dirty gin martinis are not as popular as they should be. If you love a dirty martini but have only tried it with vodka, you're missing out. In a vodka martini, all you get is the flavor of olive brine. But in this version, when the juniper and other aromatics in the gin blend with the briny taste of olives, you're creating a complex new flavor. For the olive brine, you can use the liquid from that jar of olives in your fridge.

Chill a coupe glass by filling with ice water, and empty the cold glass. Get out that mixing glass, and add the gin, olive brine, vermouth, and ice cubes. Stir and strain into the coupe glass. You can drop in a single olive for garnish, or, if you're the snacking type, skewer a few, and perch them on the edge of the glass.

CHAPTER 3

DRINKING WITH A CROWD

When you need to entertain a large group, this section has you covered. These recipes can be scaled up or down for any number of guests, so if you want to bring something other than the usual bottle of wine to a dinner party, or need to serve fifty guests at your friend's baby shower, you'll be prepared.

SURPRISE YOUR FRIENDS!
BEST DRINK TO SNEAK INTO A MOVIE THEATER:
HANKY-PANKY

**4 OZ [120 ML]
FERNET-BRANCA**

**4 OZ [120 ML] CARPANO
ANTICA FORMULA
SWEET VERMOUTH**

4 OZ [120 ML] GIN

**8 DASHES ORANGE
BITTERS**

Serves 4

Decant this easy-as-pie drink into whatever subterfuge-friendly vessels you have on hand. Depending on how strict your local cinema is, you can use flasks, thermoses, even a coffee cup. Just make sure you bring enough for everyone. You can sip on this as is, or spike an icy movie theater Coke for a smoother variation on the classic Argentinian favorite, Fernet and Coke.

In a pitcher—or measuring cup, anything with a spout, really—combine the Fernet, Antica, gin, and orange bitters. Give it all a good stir and pour into your waiting containers. (You'll definitely need a small funnel for pitcher-to-flask transfer.) Throw the flasks in your purse, and you're good to go.

MULTIPURPOSE PUNCH:
BING CHERRY VODKA LIME RICKEYS FOR ALL

INFUSED VODKA

ONE 4-OZ [115-G] BAG DRIED BING, OR OTHER TART, CHERRIES

2 CUPS [480 ML] VODKA

PUNCH

1 QT [960 ML] RAINBOW SHERBET

1 CUP[240 ML] FRESHLY SQUEEZED LIME JUICE

2 CUPS [480 ML] GINGER ALE

½ OZ [15 ML] ORANGE BLOSSOM WATER (OPTIONAL)

10 LEMON WHEELS (4 TO 5 LEMONS; SEE PAGE 23)

Serves 10

When you have a lot of people to serve, making a punch is never a bad idea. This one is playful and refreshing, and can be served any time of day. Marrying sherbet with a sophisticated homemade vodka infusion updates an old-fashioned party favorite. Using a high-quality ginger ale, such as Reed's, is also key; we promise you'll be able to tell the difference. If you can't find orange blossom water, don't worry about it. This punch will still be spectacular.

To make the infused vodka: Put the cherries in a clean 1-qt [960-ml] mason jar. Pour in the vodka, cap the jar, and shake. Refrigerate overnight. Strain out the cherries, and store the vodka until you're ready to start the punch. (The infused vodka can be made 1 day in advance and stored, covered, in the fridge.)

To make the punch; Take the sherbet out of the freezer to thaw slightly as you track down your punch bowl and assemble your ingredients. Pour the lime juice, ginger ale, and orange blossom water into the punch bowl. Add the infused vodka (you should have about 2½ cups [600 ml].

Hopefully, by now your sherbet is soft enough to scoop. If not, give it some more time. Float scoops of the sherbet on top of the punch, and gently stir the whole shebang with your serving ladle, being careful to preserve the iceberg layer of sherbet, which will naturally set on the surface.

When serving, make sure each punch glass gets a good amount of liquid and sherbet—there should be two layers in every glass. Garnish with a lemon wheel perched on the rim of each glass.

BE THE TOAST OF THE BACHELORETTE PARTY:
CHAMOYADA JELL-O SHOT LIME SLICES

6 LIMES

6 OZ [180 ML] TEQUILA OR VODKA

½ OZ [15 ML] CHAMOY PLUM SAUCE

1½ TBSP GELATIN

1¼ CUPS [300 ML] MANGO NECTAR

4 OZ [120 ML] AGAVE NECTAR

TAJIN CLASSICO CHILE-LIME-SALT SEASONING FOR GARNISH

Serves 12 to 15

This recipe is the definition of fun. It's colorful, it's a conversation starter, and best of all, it's portable. These gorgeous slices of party spirit are inspired by *chamoyada*, a popular Mexican treat made with mango sorbet that's sweet and spicy at the same time. The slices taste as good as they look, and can be made with tequila or vodka.

This is one of the more tedious recipes to make, but the payoff will be well worth your efforts, including the job of hollowing out all of those lime halves.

Prepare your limes: Cut each one in half, lengthwise. Juice two of the limes in a separate bowl and reserve for later. Under cold running water, carefully flip them inside out and tear out all the lime flesh from each half. Flip each rind back right-side out, leaving an empty little lime "bowl" with a fine layer of pith.

CONTINUED

If you have a mini-muffin tin to hold the limes, great. If not, place the rinds on a tray and support them with aluminum foil, so they are level and stable for filling. Set the tin or tray aside and prepare the filling.

In a large measuring cup—or any container with a pour spout—stir together the tequila (or vodka), lime juice, and plum sauce. Sprinkle in the gelatin while whisking the mixture.

In a small saucepan, heat the mango nectar and agave just to a simmer. When it bubbles around the edges (this will happen in 1 or 2 minutes, so watch it closely), remove from the heat, and whisk into the tequila-lime mixture until combined. Carefully fill the prepared lime rinds, and refrigerate for at least 3 hours, until the gelatin has set.

When you're ready to party, cut the lime cups in half, to create gemlike wedges. Arrange on a serving platter, and garnish with a sprinkle of Tajin seasoning over the tops. (You can make these 1 day before your party and store, covered, in the fridge.)

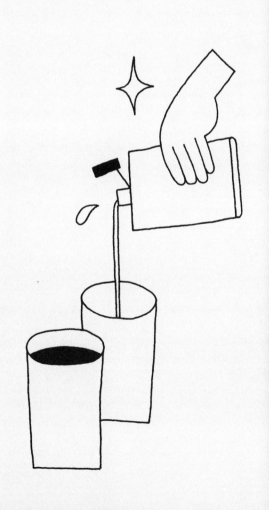

THE DRINK TO BRING TO A BEACH PICNIC:
VINO VERANO

GARNISHES ON THE GO (OPTIONAL)

8 FRESH MINT SPRIGS

8 LEMON WHEELS (3 TO 4 LEMONS; SEE PAGE 23)

1 BUNCH (ABOUT 2 OZ [55 G]) FRESH MINT

2 CUPS [480 ML] VODKA

2 CUPS [480 ML] FRESHLY SQUEEZED LEMON JUICE (ABOUT 8 TO 10 LEMONS)

1 CUP [240 ML] AGAVE NECTAR

ONE 750-ML BOTTLE RED WINE (ANY KIND YOU LIKE)

Serves 8

This version of a Tinto de Verano is meant to be shared. Make the boozy mint lemonade and keep it cool in a thermos. Then, add the wine and finishing touches at the beach. Don't forget to throw a bag of ice in your cooler for the drinks. (Crappy bodega ice is actually best for this.) And remember to bring straws and plastic cups!

To prep the extra-fancy garnishes, if using: Take a sprig and gently grasp the top leaf. Carefully strip the lower leaves, preserving the topmost, delicate five to seven leaves. You should be left with what resembles a "mint flower." Break off the end of the stem. Repeat with the remaining mint. Wrap the mint flowers in a damp paper towel and put into a plastic bag. Keep the lemon wheels in a separate plastic bag. Refrigerate until ready to use.

CONTINUED

For the drinks, pluck off all the mint leaves, discarding the stems. Shred the leaves with your hands to release essential oils and enhance the mint flavor. Put the mint in a large, clean thermos and add the vodka and lemon juice. Mix in the agave, cover, and put the thermos in the fridge.

When you get to the beach, fill a plastic cup about a third of the way with your boozy thermos lemonade. Add a ton of ice, packing the cup to the top. If you made that Dark and Stormy (page 58) and floated the rum on top, you can picture what we're doing here with the wine. Add 2 straws, or coffee stirrers, to your cup and carefully add 2 oz [60 ml] of red wine, or enough to fill the glass to create that two-tone effect.

Mix, enjoy, repeat, and feel the envy of your less-prepared fellow beach-goers. This recipe doubles easily in case you feel like sharing.

If you prepped the fancy garnishes: Drop 1 lemon wheel against the side of each glass, and tuck 1 mint flower next to it.

ELEVATION NOTE: Try making this with rosé for a lighter, albeit less visually striking, cocktail.

ICE MYTHS

Ice can be impressive, majestic, and beautifully prepared, but the only requirement ice has to fulfill is being cold. And no matter how beautiful it is, if you don't have enough, you won't have a cocktail. You'll always need more ice than you think, so having multiple ice trays filled and ready to use is essential for any home bar.

Don't worry about blowing your disposable income on fancy molds or ice chisels—just buy a couple of extra ice cube trays. Because ultimately, ice is ice, and will do the job of chilling your beverage no matter what shape it's in. The theatrics of ice picks and chisels can be entertaining, but I've never enjoyed an old-fashioned with a single giant ball of ice in it that numbs my mouth whenever I take a sip.

Sangria became a
favorite of mine
when I discovered
bottomless brunches.
It's sweet and light, but it
gets the job done.

MORGAN JERKINS, AUTHOR

SANGRIA

ICE CUBES

ONE 750 ML BOTTLE
OF RED WINE

2 OZ [60 ML] APPLE
BRANDY

2 OZ [60 ML] SIMPLE
SYRUP (SEE PAGE 108)

1 APPLE, CHOPPED

½ CUP [100 G] BERRIES
OF YOUR CHOICE (WE
RECOMMEND RASPBERRIES,
SLICED STRAWBERRIES,
OR EVEN CHERRIES)

1 ORANGE,
SLICED INTO WHEELS

1 LIME,
SLICED INTO WHEELS

1 LEMON,
SLICED INTO WHEELS

Serves 4-6

There is a widespread myth that says it's ok to use old, opened red wine in a sangria recipe, but we certainly don't recommend it. It's perfectly fine to use a cheaper red wine—in fact, avoid using something fancy—because this recipe contains so many additional fruit flavors. This recipe should be a template; feel free to riff on this in any way that's convenient or preferable to you.

It'll be easiest to build this right in the pitcher you plan to serve it in. Add all of the fruit, simple syrup, and brandy to the bottom of the pitcher. Pour in the red wine and stir to combine. Let the flavors meld in the fridge overnight (10 to 12 hours). When you're ready to serve, fill some wineglasses with ice, and pour in the sangria. This drink is effortlessly beautiful; all of that fruit is the loveliest garnish.

CHAPTER 4

DRINKING TO GET OVER ... SO MANY THINGS

Was someone, anyone, terrible to you? Did something, anything, not work out the way you planned? Disappointed? Enraged? Over it? We've been there, and these drinks sure help to smooth out those inevitable rough patches.

YOU DUMPED HIM/HER/THEM:
THE LAST WORD

1 OZ [30 ML] GIN

1 OZ [30 ML] GREEN CHARTREUSE

1 OZ [30 ML] FRESHLY SQUEEZED LIME JUICE

1 OZ [30 ML] MARASCHINO LIQUEUR

ICE CUBES

1 FRESH MINT LEAF

Serves 1

This classic cocktail has not only the best name but also one of the simplest preparations. Regardless of who said what, you can rest assured that you're getting the last word with this drink. If you don't love gin, try substituting your favorite spirit. This drink should be all about you. For the Maraschino liqueur, we like Luxardo.

Chill a coupe glass by filling it with ice water, and set aside. Take out your shaking tins, and add all the liquid ingredients to the larger one. Throw in 5 to 7 ice cubes and shake your anger out at your ex for as long as you need (but at least for 30 seconds.)

After you separate the tins, pop the Hawthorne strainer over the one with the liquid . Empty the now-cold coupe glass and with one hand, hold your small chinois strainer over the glass while you pour the cocktail into it.

Traditionally, this drink has no garnish, but if you're feeling down and a garnish would cheer you up, float the mint leaf on top for a fragrant and beautiful finishing touch that complements the herbaceous green Chartreuse.

WHEN YOU NEED A BREAK FROM THE WORLD:
FROZEN PAINKILLER

1¼ CUPS [300 ML] RUM

4 OZ [120 ML] COCONUT CREAM

2 OZ [60 ML] FRESHLY SQUEEZED ORANGE JUICE

1¼ CUPS [300 ML] PINEAPPLE JUICE

1 TSP GROUND NUTMEG, PLUS A PINCH FOR GARNISH

3 CUPS ICE

Serves 5 to 6

The painkiller does what it promises, and with its tropical, coconut notes—it's a variation on a piña colada—it simultaneously lifts your mood as it dulls your pain. This is one of our most popular summer drinks, and we guarantee that no matter where you serve it, people will ask for the recipe. We like British Navy Pusser's rum here. It's still made according to the original Royal Navy recipe, and is a blend of five different West Indian rums. For the coconut cream, we use Coco Lopez, which has the right balance of sweetness and coconut flavor.

If your blender is small, you can build half, or even a third of the recipe at a time. Otherwise, put all of these ingredients—except the ice—in a blender and blend on high until the mixture is combined. Add the ice, and blend until it's uniformly thick and smooth.

Pour into whatever glasses you prefer—for a playful twist, we use 12-oz [360-ml] brown medicine bottles at our bars. The drink will do the job, regardless of the vessel. To garnish, sprinkle with a light layer of nutmeg.

IS YOUR BOSS AN ASSHOLE?
GREEN CHARTREUSE AND FERNET SHOTS

1 OZ [30 ML] GREEN CHARTREUSE

1 OZ [30 ML] FERNET-BRANCA

Serves 2

Did you have A Day? These shots will turn it around in an instant. Kick off the weekend with one of these and a commiserating coworker or two, and take team building to the next level.

You won't need a shaking tin for these—you can mix up these shots right in the glass. Take out two shot glasses, or rocks glasses in a pinch. Using a ½-oz [15-ml] jigger, pour half the Fernet and the green Chartreuse into each glass. That is literally it. Enjoy!

ELEVATION NOTE: Pour the green Chartreuse into your shot glasses first. Add the Fernet next, as carefully as possible, floating it on top for a two-toned effect.

WHEN YOU FIND OUT SOMEBODY YOU LIKE VOTED FOR TRUMP:
DRAGON FRUIT RUM, RED PEPPER, AND PEACH DAQUIRI

---

2 OZ [60 ML] DRAGON FRUIT RUM (RECIPE FOLLOWS)

3/4 OZ [20 ML] COCONUT PEPPER SYRUP (RECIPE FOLLOWS)

3/4 OZ [20 ML] FRESHLY SQUEEZED LIME JUICE

3/4 OZ [20 ML] DIMMI LIQUEUR

2 DASHES LIME BITTERS

5 TO 7 ICE CUBES

1/4 CUP [50 G] ORGANIC CANE SUGAR

1 1/4 TSP BLACK SALT

Serves 1

Organize your thoughts and summon your proverbial dragons with a little help from this bracing and restorative cocktail. We promise you'll find the right balance of enraged and productive, to get the show on the road and make a better world possible. This drink pairs beautifully with calling your representatives, or planning your own campaign for public office. You can make it anytime the news is particularly brutal. Dimmi liqueur is Northern Italy's citrusy and licorice-y answer to absinthe.

When your infused rum and syrup are ready to use, chill a large rocks glass by filling it with ice water, and set aside. Take out your shaking tin and add the rum, syrup, lime juice, Dimmi liqueur, and lime bitters. Throw in 5 to 7 ice cubes and go to town, shaking for at least 30 seconds.

CONTINUED

Empty out your glass. Quickly combine the sugar and black salt in a shallow saucer, and press the rim of your chilled glass into the mixture, rolling it where needed for an even coating. Fill the glass with ice, being careful not to disrupt the action on the rim.

Double strain the cocktail into the glass (see page 21), and you're done!

DRAGON FRUIT RUM

4 OZ [115 G] DRIED
ORGANIC RED
DRAGON FRUIT

2 CUPS [480 ML]
WHITE RUM

Makes 2 cups
[480 ml]

In a clean 1-pt [480-ml] mason jar, combine the dragon fruit and rum. Cover, and refrigerate for 1 hour. Strain out the dragon fruit and make this drink happen. (The infused rum will keep, covered, in the fridge for 2 to 3 weeks.)

COCONUT PEPPER SYRUP

1 OZ DRIED RED PEPPER
FLAKES

1/2 CUP [30 G] SWEETENED
DRIED COCONUT FLAKES,
GROUND INTO A POWDER

1 CUP [200 G] ORGANIC
CANE SUGAR

1 CUP [240 ML] BOILING
WATER

Makes 2 cups

Combine all ingredients in a mason jar, cap it, and shake well, until the sugar has dissolved. Leave the jar in the fridge overnight, or for at least 8 hours. Strain into a clean container and refrigerate until you're ready to mix. (The syrup will keep, covered, in the fridge for 3 to 5 days.)

THE TRUTH
ABOUT VERMOUTH

Vermouth should always, always be refrigerated. This fortified wine will last for up to 3 months if it's properly cared for. So once you open a bottle, put it in the fridge immediately. There are two types, dry and sweet. Our favorite brand of dry vermouth is Noilly Prat extra dry, but other brands in the same price range are also good bets.

Sweet vermouth is a completely different story. As far as we're concerned, there is one brand and one brand only: Carpano Antica Formula. This Italian vermouth is the ne plus ultra of vermouths—it's rich, balanced, and it brings out the best in the spirits it pairs with.

WINE

...

I fear that my drinking habits may sound lazily alcoholic—I am unpicky to the point of absurdity. It's not that I drink *everything*—I really only drink wine, with the occasional beer, but in both cases, my tastes remain as inchoate as that of a college freshman. When drinking red, I like pinot noir, but is that because I saw the movie *Sideways* at an impressionable moment? When drinking white, I like sauvignon blanc, but couldn't really tell you why. To play it safe, I suppose I should just drink bottles of Veuve Cliquot, which is of course the only necessary beverage to have on hand, other than La Croix Lime.

EMMA STRAUB, AUTHOR

AN IMPOSSIBLY SHORT
WORD ON WINE

We can't really tell you anything new about wine in one page, but we can offer a couple of suggestions about serving it along with—or in lieu of—cocktails. Not everybody wants a cocktail all of the time. I like to offer sparkling wine at the beginning of a meal or night, a muscadet or (Liz Lemon's favorite) pinot grigio at a summer happy hour, or a light people-pleasing red, like a pinot noir or primitivo in the cooler months. But, there are lots of cocktails made with wine—and we provide many recipes including it. See pages 47 and 182 for more.

CHAPTER 5

DRINKING WITH FAMILY

Sometimes the cocktails you need most of all are the cocktails you can enjoy with your relatives. Oil up even the stiffest of family affairs with these welcoming drinks.

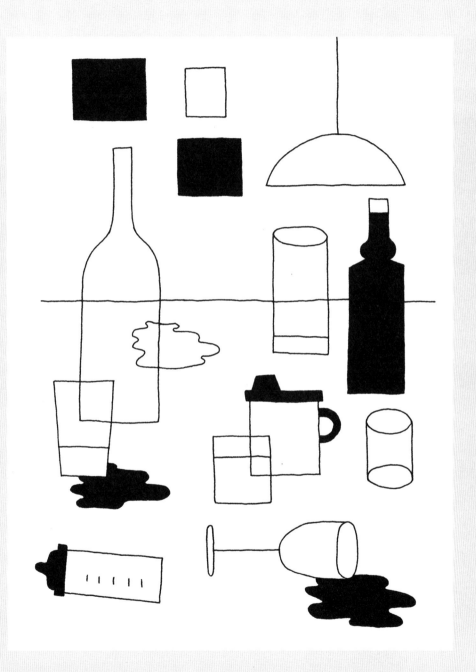

EGGNOG WITH NUTMEG BOURBON

---

3 WHOLE NUTMEGS

1½ TO 2 CUPS [360 TO 480 ML] BOURBON

8 ORGANIC EGGS (PASTEURIZED ARE OKAY IF FAMILY MEMBERS DON'T CONSUME RAW EGGS)

⅔ CUP PLUS 1 TBSP [145 G] ORGANIC CANE SUGAR

4 CUPS [960 ML] ORGANIC WHOLE CREAM-LINE MILK

2 CUPS [480 ML] ORGANIC HEAVY CREAM

Serves 10 to 12

When holiday season is upon you, instead of mixing drinks for each of your guests, simplify your entertaining life with this stunning winter punch. It's nothing like the saccharine-sweet, store-bought eggnog you may have been subjected to in the past. All of the fresh ingredients are organic, and instead of using rum, we use bourbon. Your dad won't even know what hit him. Just give yourself plenty of time to prepare the eggnog. You'll need to infuse the bourbon overnight, and allow a few hours the day of your holiday to chill before serving.

The night before you plan to serve this, crack open the nutmegs with a mallet or heavy book, and put in a clean, 1-pt [480-ml] mason jar. Pour in the bourbon, cover, and refrigerate overnight, for at least six hours.

Strain the bourbon and set aside. Separate the eggs into two large mixing bowls. To the yolks, add ⅔ cup [130 g] of the sugar, the milk, and cream. Whisk for 1 or 2 minutes, until uniformly combined, and add 1½ cups

[360 ml] of the bourbon. (Keep the extra bourbon on call in case a couple of your guests want to strengthen their drinks.) Put the bowl in the fridge.

Using a clean whisk or an electric hand mixer, whip the egg whites until soft peaks form. Slowly add the remaining sugar as you go. Take out your punch bowl. Carefully pour in the chilled yolk mixture first, and then slowly but thoroughly, fold in the whites. Refrigerate the whole shebang until completely chilled, about 2 to 3 hours. You'll know it's ready when you see a snowy layer of meringue floating on the top.

Using a ladle, serve in punch glasses or mugs, pouring an equal amount of the custard and meringue into each serving.

ELEVATION NOTE: To spice this up, slice 2 to 3 dried chipotle peppers and add to your nutmeg-infused bourbon.

BEST DRINK TO MAKE YOUR MOM:
COSMO

2 OZ [60 ML] OF YOUR MOM'S FAVORITE VODKA

5 TO 7 ICE CUBES

¾ OZ [20 ML] FRESHLY SQUEEZED LIME JUICE

¾ OZ [20 ML] COINTREAU

½ OZ [15 ML] SWEETENED CRANBERRY JUICE

1 LIME WHEEL (SEE PAGE 23)

1 STRIP ORANGE ZEST (OPTIONAL; SEE PAGE 22)

¼ CUP [60 ML] STRONG HIBISCUS TEA, COOLED TO ROOM TEMPERATURE (OPTIONAL)

Serves 1

Sometimes your mom just wants a Cosmo; I know mine does. She's probably used to getting it *Sex in the City*–style, in a comically over-sized martini glass (which she's guaranteed to spill immediately, thanks to the poor design) made with overly sweet, subpar ingredi-ents. Make this drink, and her day, with the best possible ingredi-ents, and serve it in an elegant coupe.

Chill a coupe glass by filling it with ice water, and set aside. While the glass is frosting up, fix the drink.

Pour the vodka into a shaking tin. Add 5 to 7 ice cubes. Pour in the lime and cranberry juice, and the Cointreau, too. Shake for about 30 seconds. Toss the ice water from the coupe glass. Separate the shaking tins, making sure all of the liquid is in the larger tin, and double strain the Cosmo into the glass (see page 21), to make it the smoothest one your mom will ever drink.

CONTINUED

To garnish, perch the lime wheel on the rim of the glass. If you want to fancy it up, zest the orange peel over the surface of the drink and set it on the rim beside the lime wheel. If you wish, tint the lime wheel pink by dipping it in the tea.

ELEVATION NOTE: Using an atomizer, spritz a mist of rose water over the top of the garnished drink. This elegant and fragrant finishing touch might just convince your mom to order something more adventurous the next time she's out.

BEST DRINK TO MAKE YOUR GRANDMA:
SAZERAC

1½ TSP ABSINTHE

ICE CUBES

2 OZ [60 ML] RYE

4 DASHES PEYCHAUD'S
BITTERS

2 DASHES ANGOSTURA
BITTERS

1½ TSP SIMPLE
SYRUP, HOMEMADE
(RECIPE FOLLOWS)

1 STRIP LEMON ZEST
(SEE PAGE 22)

Serves 1

Grandparents are notorious for ordering spirit-forward drinks; in our experience, Manhattans, Negronis, and martinis are extremely popular with the senior set. If your grandmother is anything like mine was, she'll appreciate this traditional New Orleans variation on an old-fashioned.

Pour the absinthe into a rocks glass, add 2 ice cubes, and swirl around, thoroughly coating the inside of the glass. Let that sit while you prepare the rest of the Sazerac in a mixing glass—a 1-pt [480-ml] glass works great.

Pour the rye into your mixing glass. Add the Peychaud's bitters, Angostura bitters, and simple syrup. Fill your mixing glass with ice and stir continuously for 45 seconds to a minute.

CONTINUED

Go back to your rocks glass and swirl absinthe a few more times; it should be an opaque light green. Dump out the ice and absinthe, and strain the rye and bitters into the glass. Zest with the lemon peel, and discard.

ELEVATION NOTE: Swap out the plain rye for caraway-infused rye, which I'll tell you how to make right now! Add ½ cup plus 1 Tbsp [60 g] of whole caraway seeds to a 1-pt [480-ml] mason jar. Fill the jar with rye whisky, twist on the lid, and refrigerate overnight. Strain through a coffee filter–lined funnel into a clean mason jar or bottle. You can use this caraway rye for anything you want, or even give it as a gift, but you really need to try it in a Sazerac. (The infused rye will keep, covered, in the fridge for 2 to 3 weeks.)

SIMPLE SYRUP

1 CUP [200 G]
ORGANIC CANE SUGAR

1 CUP [240 ML]
BOILING HOT WATER

Makes 1½ cups

Add the sugar to a 1-pt [480-ml] mason jar. Pour the water over it, cap the jar, and shake vigorously until the sugar has dissolved. You can use this right away, or, uncap and cool to room temperature. You can multiply this recipe to your heart's content. (The syrup will keep, covered, in the fridge for up to 1 week.)

WHAT TO MAKE WHEN YOU WANT TO IMPRESS SOMEONE ELSE'S FAMILY:
APEROL SPRITZ

ICE CUBES

3 OZ [90 ML] APEROL

1½ CUPS [360 ML] PROSECCO

6 OZ [[180 ML] SODA WATER

6 STRIPS ORANGE ZEST (SEE PAGE 22)

Serves 6

If you haven't tried this iconic European vacation classic, you're in for a real treat. The vibrant sunset color makes an impressive presentation, and the fruity effervescence of this cocktail ensures it's a festive crowd-pleaser. It will put anyone at ease, even a room full of people who don't know each other. It's also a great gateway cocktail for less adventurous drinkers.

Take out six champagne flutes—or whatever glasses you have that match. Wineglasses work great. This is supereasy because there's no shaking involved, and you can recruit help from anyone who's just standing around. Fill all of the glasses with ice. To each glass, add ½ oz [15 ml] of Aperol and 2 oz [60 ml] of prosecco, and top with 1 oz [30 ml] of soda water.

Zest with a fragrant strip of orange peel, and then drop it in the glass to garnish. Pass the drinks around, and prepare to be popular.

ELEVATION NOTE: Instead of using prosecco, try making this with sparkling rosé.

THE IMPORTANCE OF BUBBLES

There are currently many fancy artisanal tonic and soda waters on the market. These are often made with organic ingredients and no high-fructose corn syrup. And they are being marketed to cocktail enthusiasts and bars and restaurants as a more sophisticated alternative to run-of-the-mill soda and tonic waters.

The sad news is, while the ingredients are great, the bubbles are not. The carbonation in these specialty offerings is rarely sufficient when mixed with other spirits. You want the most concentrated, even aggressively carbonated mixers you can get your hands on. No matter what, you're always adding these to more liquid, and the carbonation will always be diluted. So start with the bubbliest soda water out there, even if it's the humblest one on the shelf.

I love the mix of salty and sweet, the texture of the grains between my mouth and the glass. It makes me feel more present as I drink, more alert to the world around me, taking it all in with more than a few grains of salt.

LAUREN ELKIN, AUTHOR

MARGARITA

KOSHER SALT FOR
COATING THE RIM

2 LIME WEDGES, PLUS
¾ OZ [20 ML] FRESHLY
SQUEEZED LIME JUICE

2 OZ [60 ML] TEQUILA

1½ TSP AGAVE NECTAR

2 DASHES ORANGE
BITTERS

ICE CUBES

1 LIME WHEEL
(SEE PAGE 23)

1 STRAW

Serves 1

You'll find all of the classic margarita flavors in this recipe—the salt! the lime! the tequila!—but our recipe is not entirely faithful to the classic because of the added lime wedge to the shaking process. It adds just the right amount of bitterness for balance, and the shaking activates and incorporates all of the subtle flavors the lime rind has to offer.

Put a thin layer of salt in a shallow saucer. Run a wedge of lime around the rim of a large rocks glass and press the rim into the salt to coat (see page 24). In a shaking tin, combine the tequila, lime juice, agave, orange bitters, and the remaining lime wedge. Throw in 5 to 7 ice cubes and shake for at least 30 seconds. Fill your salted-rimmed glass with ice, and strain the margarita into the glass. Garnish with the lime wheel and a straw, and enjoy!

CHAPTER 6

DRINKING TO GET SEXY

Inviting a special (or not-so-special) someone over for the first time? Making a drink for the person you've been married to for over a decade? Getting your bearings after a big fight? These seductive drinks will impress, entice, and enhance all of your romantic possibilities, even if you're getting sexy alone.

SETTING THE MOOD AKA ROSE PETALS ON THE BED AND IN YOUR GLASS:
ROSE TEQUILA SLEEPER

─────────

4 OZ [120 ML] BLANCO TEQUILA

1½ OZ [45 ML] FRESHLY SQUEEZED LEMON JUICE

1½ OZ [45 ML] ST. GERMAIN ELDERFLOWER LIQUEUR

¾ OZ [30 ML] CRÈME DE VIOLETTE

1 TBSP GOOD HONEY, PREFERABLY WILDFLOWER

2 EGG WHITES

5 TO 7 ICE CUBES

2 SPRAYS ATOMIZED ROSE WATER (SEE NOTE BELOW)

DRIED OR FRESH ROSE PETALS FOR GARNISH

─────────

Serves 2

This is the cocktail equivalent of your best underwear, or your sexiest playlist. When you want to maximize allure, serve up this statuesque drink. The romance factor is amplified by the sensual texture and the marbled, petal-pink garnish.

If you don't have an atomizer, add a drop of rosewater with the rest of the ingredients before mixing.

Take out your shaking tin and add the tequila, lemon juice, St. Germain, crème de violette, honey, and egg whites. Without adding ice, shake for 30 to 45 seconds—this is called dry shaking. Separate your tins, throw in 5 to 7 ice cubes, and shake again, this time for about 1 minute.

Take out your two most elegant coupe glasses, and double strain the cocktail into the glasses (see page 21). The drink should look frothy and luminous. Spritz each glass with rose water, and garnish by gently floating a few rose petals on top, being careful not to disturb the layers of the drink.

BEST DRINK FOR MAKING UP:
CUCUMBER, MINT, AND ABSINTHE JULEP

---

10 FRESH MINT LEAVES

10 CUCUMBER SLICES, PLUS 6 FOR GARNISH (ABOUT 2 CUCUMBERS)

2 WHITE SUGAR CUBES

6½ OZ [195 ML] SODA WATER

1½ OZ [45 ML] ABSINTHE

1½ OZ [45 ML] PERNOD

½ OZ [15 ML] GREEN CHARTREUSE

1½ OZ [45 ML] FRESHLY SQUEEZED LIME JUICE

ICE CUBES, CRUSHED OR CRACKED WITH A BLENDER OR MALLET

2 FRESH MINT SPRIGS

4 SHORT STRAWS

Serves 2

This is the most refreshing and bracing reimagining of a mint julep in the entire universe. Anyone will forgive you if you're serving up this drink.

Take out two of your nicest looking julep tins and add 5 mint leaves and 5 cucumber slices to each one. Toss 1 sugar cube into each tin, and add 1½ tsp (a capful) of soda water. Muddle the contents of both tins thoroughly, until you've created a sweet, minty, cucumber-laced mash. Divide the absinthe, Pernod, green Chartreuse, and lime juice between the two tins.

CONTINUED

Fill the tins with cracked or crushed ice—whoever is being apologized to should do the crushing to resolve any lingering angst. But before each tin is completely filled, fan 3 cucumber slices along the top edge of the rim. Add more ice, securing the fan in place. Pour 3 oz [90 ml] of soda into each tin, and garnish with 2 short straws and 1 mint sprig.

WHEN STAYING IN IS BETTER THAN GOING OUT:
ROSEMARY AND APPLE RYE SOUR

4 SPRIGS FRESH ROSEMARY

2 TBSP GOOD QUALITY HONEY

4 OZ [120 ML] RYE

2 OZ [60 ML] FRESHLY SQUEEZED LEMON JUICE

4 DASHES SMOKED CHILE BITTERS

ICE CUBES

4 OZ [120 ML] SPARKLING CIDER

2 STRAWS

Serves 2

When the fall weather hits and all you want to do is stay in with your sweetheart—or home alone—make a couple of these to drink under the covers. This cocktail is cider-y and autumnal, and gets the blood flowing in all the right ways.

Take out your shaking tins. Strip the leaves off 2 sprigs of the rosemary, letting the leaves fall into the smaller tin. (Discard the stems.) Add the honey, rye, lemon juice, and smoked chile bitters. Throw in 5 to 7 ice cubes and shake hard for about 45 seconds so that you break up all of that spicy and fragrant rosemary.

Fill two tall glasses with ice, and double strain, pouring half the contents of the shaking tin into each one (see page 21). The glasses should be about two-thirds full. Top with the sparkling cider. Clap the remaining 2 rosemary sprigs between your hands to release the essential oils to perfume the glass, and garnish each drink with a sprig and a straw.

THE DRINK TO MAKE FOR A ONE-NIGHT STAND:
TEQUILA AND HABANERO SOUR

4 OZ [120 ML] BLANCO TEQUILA

2 OZ [60 ML] FRESHLY SQUEEZED LEMON JUICE

1½ OZ [45 ML] AGAVE NECTAR

2 DASHES HABANERO HOT SAUCE

ICE CUBES

2 LEMON WHEELS (SEE PAGE 23)

Serves 2

Make the first move by making this drink. This tequila sour has just the right amount of spice to spark an engaging conversation and really heat things up. Some bartenders will tell you that tequila and lemon don't mix, but that's simply not true, as you'll see once you try one of these. This is what we call double batching, basically just making two drinks at once in the same shaker to save time.

Take out two rocks glasses and your shaking tin. Pour the tequila, lemon juice, and agave into the tin. Add the hot sauce and 5 to 7 ice cubes. You might want to shake this a little longer than usual, closer to 45 seconds, since you're making two drinks at once.

Throw a few ice cubes into each rocks glass, and separate your shaking tin. Pop on that Hawthorne strainer and pour an equal amount into each glass. Garnish with a lemon wheel, and you're done!

ELEVATION NOTE: This drink is great as is, but goes to the next level when made with your own cilantro-infused tequila. If you're a cilantro fan, this tequila is great to have on hand for any beverage. If you're one of those cilantro-tastes-like-soap-to-me people, you should still consider giving this a try. The infusion in alcohol seems to diffuse that unsavory element.

Chop up 1 bunch of cilantro and put in any 1-L container. (Don't worry about the stems; everything will be strained out later.) Pour in a bottle of your favorite blanco tequila (and save the bottle and cap!). Cover the container and refrigerate overnight. In the morning, pour through your finest chinois strainer into the original bottle. There should be no bits of cilantro in the liquid, so strain twice if you must. (The infused tequila will keep, covered, in the fridge for up to 1 week.)

AVIATION

...

This cocktail is so fresh and so feminine. It's the kind of drink you want to have during a date. I think flavors in a cocktail can change your mood, and this cocktail puts me in a sensual and seductive mood.

I also really love the way it looks. It doesn't look like there's alcohol in it—the color is beautiful, very chic. I've also always loved these coupe cocktail glasses because in France, I learned that it was made by the shape of women's breasts. So I feel like I'm honoring women by drinking from this glass.

VIOLETTE, MAKEUP ARTIST

AVIATION

2 OZ [60 ML] GIN

**¾ OZ [20 ML] FRESHLY
SQUEEZED LEMON JUICE**

**½ OZ MARASCHINO
LIQUEUR**

1½ TSP CRÈME DE VIOLETTE

5 TO 7 ICE CUBES

**1 LUXARDO MARASCHINO
CHERRY**

**1 SPRAY ATOMIZED
ORANGE BLOSSOM WATER
(OPTIONAL)**

Serves 1

Violette loves the eponymous floral presence of crème de violette, which makes this drink so special. An aviation is a stylish and beautiful classic, and while not too widely known, it should not be missed. This is our version.

Combine the gin, lemon juice, Maraschino liqueur, and crème de violette in your shaking tin. Add the ice cubes and shake. Separate the tins, and double strain (see page 21) into a waiting chilled coupe glass. Drop in the Luxardo cherry, and spray your orange water across the top of the glass for an added floral fragrance. If you don't have it, no big deal! The drink is still amazing without.

THE VODKA MYTH

There is a dearth of kindness and understanding in many cocktail bars when it comes to vodka. I remember a time when nouveau speakeasies wouldn't even put vodka drinks on their menus. Some bartenders claim that it's "not really a spirit," or that "it doesn't taste like anything." None of this is true—in a methodical taste test, vodkas can range wildly in flavor profile. Some are smooth, some are peppery, some are even a little sweet. At the end of the day, vodka is a versatile spirit that can make an incredible balanced cocktail. It's your drink—if you prefer vodka, order it without embarrassment.

If you're still self-conscious about your vodka cocktail, here are some badass facts about this ancient Eastern European spirit to brandish around the bar: The original vodka cocktail was called "the cup of the white eagle." It consisted of 6½ cups [1.5 L] of vodka, and was served in Peter the Great's court to all foreign ambassadors upon their arrival in Russia. Vodka can also prevent a reaction to poison ivy, and if that's not amazing enough, it also has its own museum in St. Petersburg.

CHAPTER 7

DRINKING IN THE MORNING

Day drinking is a time-honored national pastime. Want to feel like a languid, nineteenth-century poet, or a glamorous country-house hostess? Be prepared, whether you're making brunch or are on a staycation, to dial up to festive whenever you want.

MAKE A MIMOSA YOU DIDN'T EVEN KNOW WAS POSSIBLE:
MIMOSA WITH A TWIST

1½ TSP APEROL

2 DASHES ORANGE BITTERS

2½ OZ [80 ML] FRESHLY SQUEEZED ORANGE JUICE

2½ OZ [80 ML] PROSECCO OR SPARKLING WINE

1 FRESH BASIL LEAF

1 STRIP ORANGE ZEST (SEE PAGE 22)

Serves 1

If you love brunch, then you need this recipe in your life. Freshly squeezed—and really well-strained—orange juice is a wonder. You can make just one for yourself, or enough for a table of guests; you just can't skimp on the orange juice. It must be squeezed that day—by you—and double strained to keep any trace of pulp or seeds from your glass (see page 21). We've all had those slapdash, gritty, mass-produced mimosas, but you don't have to go back to those substandard bleary mornings ever again. This mimosa takes orange flavor to another level, with surprisingly little fuss. The Aperol rinse adds complexity and depth to the drink, which at first glance may seem very basic.

Chill a coupe glass or champagne flute by filling it with ice water. Before building your drink, dump the ice water out of the glass and add the Aperol. Over the kitchen sink, rotate the glass, completely coating the inside. Toss the excess Aperol, and then go ahead and fix yourself that mimosa.

Grab your chilled, rinsed glass and add the orange bitters to the bottom. Pour in your orange juice, and top with prosecco (or other sparkling wine of your choice) and basil. You can zest the drink and discard the orange peel, or perch the twist on the rim of the glass.

ELEVATION NOTE: Try this rinse with Campari or even absinthe for subtle variations on the classic brunch drink theme.

SHOCK AND SURPRISE—
TURN A SUNDAY MORNING FAVORITE GREEN:
TOMATILLO BLOODY MARY

1 POUND [480 ML] TOMATILLOS, HUSKED, RINSED, AND JUICED

1 JALAPEÑO (ABOUT 2 OZ [55 G]), JUICED

1 LARGE GREEN APPLE (ABOUT 7 OZ [200 G]), JUICED

½ LARGE, SEEDLESS CUCUMBER (ABOUT 7 OZ [200 G]), JUICED

2 OZ [60 ML] FRESHLY SQUEEZED LIME JUICE

1 TSP HIMALAYAN SEA SALT OR KOSHER SALT

¾ OZ [20 ML] SIMPLE SYRUP, HOMEMADE (SEE PAGE 108)

ICE CUBES

1 CUP [240 ML] VODKA

4 LIME WEDGES (SEE PAGE 22)

4 STRAWS

Serves 4

If you're experiencing Bloody Mary fatigue, wake up your taste buds with our variation on the classic. Tomatillos provide a bright, zingy alternative to the standard, one-note tomato mix. You won't regret mixing up a batch of these in lieu of the usual bloodies. They will be delicious as soon as the mix is chilled, but if you let it sit overnight, the flavors will develop more fully. And you can have a leisurely morning and wait for your guests to arrive.

CONTINUED

An electric juicer is not always a part of everyone's kitchen, but it's a helpful tool for this recipe. If you don't have a juicer, and can't borrow one, don't despair. You can throw the produce in a food processor and strain out the correct amounts. Combine the tomatillo, jalapeño, apple, and cucumber juices in a pitcher.

Whisk in the lime juice, salt, and simple syrup. Refrigerate for at least 2 hours, or better, overnight.

To serve, fill four tall glasses with ice. Pour 2 oz [60 ml] of vodka into each glass, and follow that up with about 5 oz [150 ml] of the tomatillo mix (or stop pouring when the glass is full). For garnish, balance a lime wedge on the rim of each glass. Don't forget the straw!

WHEN YOU TAKE BRUNCH SERIOUSLY:
ELDERFLOWER BELLINIS

**2 OZ [60 ML]
PEACH JUICE OR
PEACH NECTAR**

**½ OZ [15 ML]
ST. GERMAIN
ELDERFLOWER
LIQUEUR**

**5 OZ [150 ML]
CHILLED PROSECCO**

**1 PERFECT FRESH
SAGE LEAF**

Serves 1

Elevate a regular old Bellini with this one easy twist. It's simple, beautiful, and unexpected. Your brunch guests won't ever want to leave.

In a large champagne flute or even a wineglass, combine the peach juice and elderflower liqueur. Give it a light stir, and slowly pour over the prosecco to fill the glass.

Float the sage leaf on the surface for garnish to evoke the feeling of drinking in a garden.

MONDAY IS COMING, SO MAKE THE MOST OF IT:
DEATH IN THE AFTERNOON

———

¾ OZ [20 ML] ABSINTHE

4 OZ [120 ML] CHILLED
PROSECCO

1 WHITE SUGAR CUBE

———

Serves 1

Stretch your Sunday afternoon with this decadent favorite, but be
prepared to go to bed early.

Add the absinthe to any style of champagne glass. Pour in your chilled
prosecco and appreciate the pearly-green color that magically appears
when you mix these two together. Drop in the sugar cube, and take
advantage of the delightful and gratifying fizz.

GOESAERT V. CLEARY

In 1948, the Supreme Court ruled in favor of a Michigan law that prohibited women from working behind the bar unless they were the wife or daughter of the bar's owner. This case relied on the argument that women bartenders would otherwise be socially and morally compromised.

It wasn't until 1976 that the decision was overruled. (A woman couldn't even open her own tab at the bar until 1974, when a single woman could finally open a credit card account in her own name without the cosigned approval of her father or husband.)

COSMOPOLITAN

...

For me, the Cosmo represents
the best of womanhood.
Multifaceted and well blended,
strong yet sweet,
and always a bit of a surprise.

There's an incredible Tangerine Cosmo
made in West Stockbridge, where the
bartender, Jeremy Kenny, was inspired
by the feminist symbolism on Passover.
The tradition began with a man
questioning the role of women in services,
comparing them to an orange on a Seder plate.
Ever since then, some Jewish people
choose to honor women by including
the fruit in Passover, to assert the
symbolic place of women in religion.

**LENORA LAPIDUS, DIRECTOR OF THE ACLU
WOMEN'S RIGHTS PROJECT**

See our Cosmo recipe on page 104.

CHAPTER 8

DRINKING WITH PEOPLE WHO DON'T DRINK

One of the loveliest and most essential features of entertaining is making everyone feel welcome and important. You should be prepared to entertain anyone, even and especially those who aren't drinking alcohol.

WHAT TO MAKE FOR YOUR PREGNANT FRIEND WHEN SHE DOESN'T WANT PEOPLE TO KNOW SHE'S PREGNANT:
BASIL, POMEGRANATE, AND BAY LEAF SODA

5 TO 7 ICE CUBES

1 TBSP POMEGRANATE SEEDS

5 FRESH BASIL LEAVES

¾ OZ [20 ML] FRESHLY SQUEEZED LIME JUICE

½ OZ [15 ML] AGAVE NECTAR

ABOUT 6 OZ [180 ML] SODA WATER OR SPARKLING WATER

2 FRESH BAY LEAVES (OR 2 MORE BASIL LEAVES)

1 STRAW

Serves 1

This is our go-to option for guests who are trying to keep pregnancy news quiet, but look and feel like they're drinking the real thing. This herbaceous soda is refreshing and beautiful, and will brighten the night of any mom-to-be. For the fizzy water, you can use plain or a flavor of your choice. We love La Croix's coconut sparkling water.

This drink is built and shaken in the tin, but no straining is required. Throw the ice cubes into your shaking tin, along with the pomegranate seeds, basil, lime juice, and agave. Shake like your life depends on it, for at least 30 seconds, to break up the basil leaves, pomegranate seeds, and ice.

Pour the whole shebang into a tall glass, and top with enough soda water to fill it. This drink is especially gorgeous because your guest will be able to see the ruby-colored flecks of the pomegranate and the bright-green basil swirling around. Garnish with the fresh bay leaves, fanned, and a straw.

JUST NOT DRINKING? THAT'S COOL:
JALAPEÑO BLACKBERRY LEMONADE

2 SLICES JALAPEÑO

**1 OZ [30 ML] FRESHLY
SQUEEZED LEMON JUICE**

4 BLACKBERRIES

**1 OZ [30 ML] SIMPLE SYRUP,
HOMEMADE (SEE PAGE 108)**

ICE CUBES

6 OZ [180 ML] SODA WATER

1 STRAW

Serves 1

This grown-up lemonade is sweet and spicy, and also turns the loveliest color. It's a sophisticated alternative to the usual, run-of-the-mill options available to anyone avoiding alcohol.

Throw 1 jalapeño slice, the lemon juice, blackberries, and simple syrup into your shaking tin, and add 5 to 7 ice cubes. Shake well, for at least 30 seconds, and strain into a tall glass filled with ice. Top with soda water. Notch the remaining jalapeño slice and perch it on the rim of the glass. Don't forget the straw.

ELEVATION NOTE: If you want to take the garnish to the next level, skewer—with a nice toothpick—first a lemon wheel, then the slice of jalapeño, and finally, a single blackberry. You could also simplify this garnish by skewering a blackberry with a bit of mint. Either way, carefully tuck the garnish between the ice and the side of the glass and enjoy!

WHEN THERE ARE LOTS OF KIDS AT YOUR THANKSGIVING:
BUTTERNUT SQUASH–HOT APPLE CIDER, IN A SLOW COOKER!
(YOU CAN ALWAYS ADD BOURBON FOR THE ADULTS . . .

4 ALLSPICE BERRIES

1½ TSP WHOLE CLOVES

4 WHOLE STAR ANISE

6 TO 8 CARDAMOM PODS

8 CUPS [2 L] ORGANIC APPLE CIDER

ONE 15-OZ CAN [430-G] ORGANIC BUTTERNUT SQUASH PUREE

GARNISHES (OPTIONAL)

¾ OZ [20 G] CINNAMON BARK, OR 6 CINNAMON STICKS, PLUS 10 CINNAMON STICKS FOR GARNISH

6 DRIED ORANGE SLICES

BOURBON FOR SERVING (OPTIONAL)

Serves 8 to 10

This recipe is so good that we urge you to buy a slow cooker, if you don't have one. The thirty bucks you spend on Amazon will be well worth the results. If you're serving this on a holiday—we always make it at Thanksgiving—using the slow cooker frees up real estate on the stove, and ensures that the drink will be warm and available all day long. But don't worry, if you can't get your hands on a slow cooker; it's just as delicious simmered in a pan.

Dust off your slow cooker (honestly, any slow cooker that won't start a fire and that can accommodate the amount of liquid in this recipe will do), and find some space on the counter. In a small bowl, combine the allspice, cloves, star anise, and cardamom. Transfer the mixture to a spice or tea ball infuser if you have one—or just a coffee filter and some kitchen twine. Pour the cider into the slow cooker and add the butternut squash puree. Whisk or stir until combined, then add the spices. Put the cinnamon and orange slices into the mixture directly.

Set the slow cooker to low for 4 to 8 hours, depending on how long you want to enjoy it. Give it at least 3 hours on low before you serve. If you're preparing this on the stove top, simmer for 30 minutes over low heat and be ready to go.

Ladle out the cider into 8-oz [240-ml] mugs, and garnish each one with a fresh cinnamon stick. Serve to the nondrinking family members as is, but feel free to add bourbon where required. It's the holidays! That caraway-infused rye you made for the Sazerac (Elevation Note, page 108) would also be great in this cider, just saying.

THE POLITE WAY TO TELL SOMEONE
TO STOP DRINKING, WITHOUT SAYING A WORD:
HIBISCUS ARNOLD PALMER

½ CUP [100 G] ORGANIC CANE SUGAR

1 CUP [240 ML] FRESHLY SQUEEZED LEMON JUICE (ABOUT 6 TO 8 LEMONS)

4 TEA BAGS OF YOUR CHOICE

2 TBSP [20 G] OF DRIED HIBISCUS FLOWERS

5 LEMONS, THINLY SLICED

ICE CUBES

8 TO 10 STRAWS

Serves 8 to 10

This drink is colorful, refreshing, and hydrating. For an additional bracing kick, use English Breakfast or any good black tea to make the iced tea; we like Earl Grey. You can also keep it caffeine-free and use an herbal blend.

If you're having a party, you can prepare and serve the lemonade and iced tea separately over ice, or mix up and garnish these Arnold Palmers one at a time, on request. This recipe doubles easily, FYI.

In a clean pitcher, mix 3½ cups [840 ml] warm water with the sugar until the sugar is dissolved. Pop this in the fridge while you juice your lemons. Add the lemon juice to the cooled sweetened water and refrigerate the lemonade until you're ready to serve.

For Part II, you'll essentially be making a batch of gorgeously magenta, unsweetened iced tea. In a medium saucepan, bring 4½ cups [1 L] of water to a simmer. Add the tea bags and hibiscus and simmer for 3 to

5 minutes. Remove from the heat and carefully remove the tea bags. Set a large chinois strainer directly over a heat-proof pitcher, and pour the mixture through, straining out all of the hibiscus leaves. Once the tea has reached room temperature, put the pitcher in the fridge.

When you're ready to assemble, gently line the bottom of each glass with 6 thin rounds of lemon, so that they overlap. Fill a glass with ice, wedging the lemon slices between the side of the glass and the ice. Add a straw now, so it doesn't disrupt the visual magic that's about to happen. Measure out 5 oz [150 ml] of lemonade and pour it into your glass. Carefully pour in 3 oz [90 ml] of the iced tea, floating it on top of the lemonade to create a vivid two-toned effect.

MANHATTAN

...

A brief history of my favorite drinks:

Age 21 to 28
(pre-NYC, across America, broke but having fun, an efficient drinker): bourbon with a beer back

28 to 31
(East Village, attempting to be a career girl): dirty martini with extra olives

31 to 40
(Brooklyn, a freelancer, now with 100 percent more bartender friends): rye Manhattan

41 to 44
(always on the road): expensive red wine from the
hotel bar at the end of the night, which I promptly bill
back to my publisher

45 on
(New Orleans, at last): cocktails with clear liquors.
I'm too old for the brown stuff now. Martinis again,
palomas, and the like. Sometimes a daiquiri on a
sunny day, while I bike around the city.

Ask me again in another five years.
I'm pretty sure I'm going to live forever.

JAMI ATTENBERG, AUTHOR

ONE OF JAMI ATTENBERG'S FAVORITES:
MANHATTAN

2½ OZ [80 ML] RYE

¾ OZ [20 ML] SWEET VERMOUTH

3 DASHES ANGOSTURA BITTERS

5 TO 7 ICE CUBES

1 LUXARDO MARASCHINO CHERRY, OR 1 STRIP LEMON ZEST (SEE PAGE 22)

Serves 1

One of the best things about Jami's favorites is that there isn't just one. It's wonderful and totally natural that a person would have multiple favorites over the course of her life, favorites that depend on her finances, where she lives, and her work schedule. A rye Manhattan is great no matter where you live, or which recipe your bartender prefers.

Combine the rye, vermouth, and bitters in your mixing glass. Throw in the ice cubes and stir it all up. Strain into a chilled coupe, skewer the cherry, and garnish the drink. Or, if you don't have one on hand, zest with the lemon peel. If you are flush with Luxardo cherries, feel free to skewer as many as you like when garnishing. No need for restraint here!

ORGEAT:
WHAT'S THAT?

Orgeat is a roasted almond and rosewater syrup. It's delicious, but time-consuming to prepare and difficult to find. It's used mostly in mai tais, and other tiki cocktails. If you ever find yourself without it, you can cheat this ingredient by adding a dash or two of almond extract to a few ounces of simple syrup. Your guests won't know the difference.

CHAPTER 9

DRINKING IN A HURRY

You don't need a full bar, or tons of time to impress anybody. These drinks can all be put together in a compressed timeline, with only a few ingredients, and are sure to surprise and stun your family, friends, and colleagues.

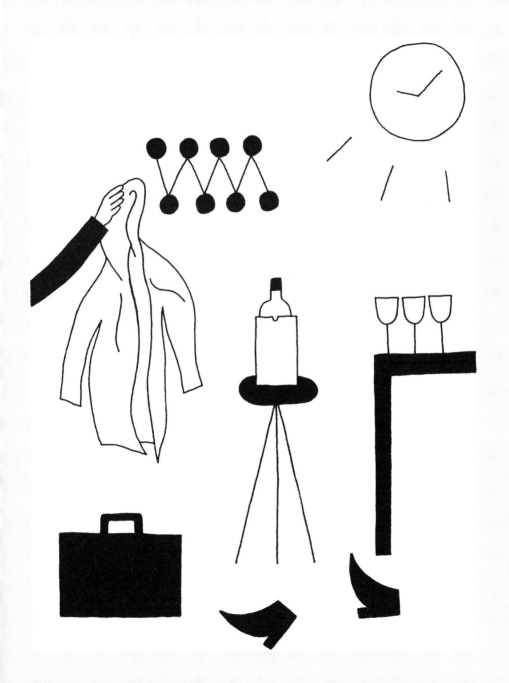

LAST-MINUTE PUNCH:
NEGRONIS FOR A GROUP

1½ CUPS [360 ML] CAMPARI

1½ CUPS [360 ML] SWEET VERMOUTH

1½ CUPS [360 ML] GIN

ICE

20 STRIPS ORANGE ZEST OR 20 ORANGE WHEELS (OPTIONAL; SEE PAGES 22–23)

Serves 20

This punch could not be simpler. Make Negronis for a crowd, and transport your family and friends to an Italian balcony in an instant. The trickiest move in this recipe is the garnish. And, while a perfectly zested orange peel is nice, it's not entirely necessary. You can easily garnish with a beautiful, jewel-like orange wheel. If you want this to be truly interactive, prepare enough strips of orange zest for all of your guests. This way, you can teach everyone how to zest and garnish their own drinks! This recipe can be scaled up or down, too; just remember to keep the same ratios. For the sweet vermouth, we recommend Carpano Antica.

Gin not your thing? Substitute rye or bourbon to make a batch of boulevardiers. For a bowl full of old pals, keep the rye or bourbon, and swap in dry vermouth for sweet.

Fill a punch bowl or pitcher with the Campari, vermouth, and gin, and stir. Keep a large container of ice nearby. Your guests can serve themselves, and ladle as much ice and punch as they like into their glasses. You can use punch glasses, or rocks glasses, or whatever you have on hand. If you want to provide garnishes, leave the orange zest or wheels beside the ice for DIY garnishing. That's it!

ELEVATION NOTE: Let's talk about Aperol. It's Campari's kinder, gentler cousin. If you don't think you're a Negroni person because you've been turned off by its bitterness in the past, try swapping out the Campari for Aperol. The drinks will still be beautifully scarlet and citrusy, but much smoother.

USE-WHATEVER-BEER-YOU-HAVE-IN-YOUR-FRIDGE:
SHANDY

**½ OZ [15 ML] SIMPLE
SYRUP, HOMEMADE
(SEE PAGE 108)**

**¾ OZ [20 ML] FRESHLY
SQUEEZED LEMON JUICE**

**ONE 12-OZ [360-ML]
CAN OR BOTTLE OF
CHILLED BEER**

Serves 1

A shandy is usually made with beer and lemonade, but there are lots of fun variations to experiment with, depending on what's available to you. Say you had a party and were left with a hodge-podge of beers; this recipe is a great way to make even the worst brands tolerable.

Pour the simple syrup into a 1-pt [480-ml] glass or beer mug, or large glass. Add the lemon juice, and then pour in your beer. That's it!

SUDDEN CELEBRATION:
CLASSIC CHAMPAGNE COCKTAIL

1 WHITE SUGAR CUBE

2 TO 3 DASHES ANGOSTURA BITTERS

5 OZ [150 ML] CHILLED CHAMPAGNE, PROSECCO, OR OTHER SPARKLING WINE

1 STRIP ORANGE ZEST (OPTIONAL; SEE PAGE 22)

Serves 1

This drink manages to be perfectly balanced, eternally classic, and incredibly impressive with only three ingredients. When your friend announces she's newly engaged, or got that promotion, you can whip these up in no time. If that isn't enough to convince you, this drink literally gets sweeter with every sip. And you can make ten of these in about the same time it will take you to make one.

Place a sugar cube in the bottom of your loveliest champagne flute. Douse it with Angostura, and let sit for a moment, until the sugar is pretty much saturated.

Pour in enough champagne to fill the glass, and prepare your toast. No need to garnish, but if you'd like, an orange zest won't go amiss.

WHEN YOUR FRIEND TEXTS "HEY, CAN YOU MAKE COCKTAILS AT MY PARTY TONIGHT?" AND YOU'RE STILL AT WORK:
MOSCOW MULES

1½ TSP DICED PEELED
FRESH GINGER

½ OZ [15 ML] FRESHLY
SQUEEZED LIME JUICE

2 OZ [60 ML] VODKA

ICE, CRUSHED OR NOT

2 OZ [60 ML] GINGER BEER

1 LIME WHEEL
(SEE PAGE 23)

1 STRAW

Serves 1

Mules are usually made with vodka, store-bought ginger beer, and lime juice. Just by adding fresh ginger to this recipe, you can transform it into something people will be talking about. So pick up a piece of ginger, along with that six-pack of ginger beer, on your way home.

Toss the ginger into a mule mug, julep tin, or any 12-oz [360-ml] glass. Muddle the ginger, and add your lime juice and vodka. Fill the glass with ice, and pour over the ginger beer. Using crushed ice is traditional, but frankly, any ice will do. Add a straw and garnish with a lime wheel.

ELEVATION NOTE: Does your friend have a crème brûlée torch? Use it to singe the surface of the lime wheel before garnishing. There's nothing quite like the fragrance of charred lime. You can use this garnish in your Dark and Stormy, too.

THE
GLASSWARE MYTH

The amount of glassware out there can be intimidating. If you tried to invest in every kind of glass that is appropriate for every kind of drink, you'd lose your mind *and* break the bank.

These cocktail recipes will adapt easily to your lifestyle, and the glassware you already have. Don't feel unprepared if you don't have a hurricane glass or a martini glass. You'll see suggestions, but use what you've got. If you make a delicious drink and spruce it up with a lovely garnish, no one will care if they're drinking a margarita out of a water glass.

I'm the first person
who has ever thought of
it. It's so good and chill
and it hits the spot.

SUNITA MANI, COMEDIAN

FERNET AND COKE

ICE CUBES

2 OZ [60 ML] FERNET

4-6 OZ [120-180 ML] COCA-COLA; WE LIKE MEXICAN COKE MADE WITHOUT CORN SYRUP

1 STRIP LEMON ZEST (OPTIONAL; SEE PAGE 23)

1 STRAW

Serves 1

This is a breeze to prepare, and a little more interesting than a typical something-and-Coke drink. Fernet is usually considered an aperitif, but you can enjoy this recipe before, during, or after any meal.

Fill a rocks glass with ice. Pour in the Fernet and top with coke. For an extra citrusy kick, zest your lemon peel over the glass and drop in for garnish. Add that straw, too.

CHAPTER 10

DRINKING WITH TIME ON YOUR SIDE

When you want to put together some mind-blowing refreshments—and you have at least 24 hours to prepare—turn to these recipes. They all require a little more planning, and a touch more effort, but they're ready to go the next day whenever you are. These drinks are dinner party gold, vacation house favorites, and most of all, they reduce hosting-related stress with all of their make-ahead possibilities.

SALTED WATERMELON ROSÉ POPSICLES

2 CUPS [480 ML] ROSÉ
WINE, CHILLED

1 CUP [240 ML] FRESH WELL-
STRAINED WATERMELON
JUICE (¼ WATERMELON
SHOULD DO THE TRICK)

4 OZ [120 ML] SIMPLE SYRUP,
HOMEMADE (SEE PAGE 108)

½ TSP GELATIN

8 PERFECT BASIL LEAVES

MALDON SEA SALT FOR
GARNISH

8 POPSICLE STICKS

Serves 8

We make Frozen Salted Watermelon Rosé for our customers all summer long—it's by far our most popular warm weather menu item. They're beautiful, incredibly easy to drink, and keep everyone cool on the hottest days of the year. Since most people don't have commercial-grade frozen margarita machines in their homes, we've translated this summer hit into popsicle form. I can assure you that these adult ices are just as beautiful, refreshing, and delicious as the originals. You'll need to buy or borrow popsicle molds if you don't already have them, ideally 4-oz [120-ml] molds or smaller.

I've made these for barbecues, picnics, and at a friend's beach house. They're a wholly unexpected treat every time. Since all the work is done the night before, you can just pop them out of the freezer, garnish, and serve. You'll be sure to delight even the crankiest, most overheated guests when you present them with these bright pink marvels. For the basil get 8 of the most beautiful, verdant leaves you can find.

CONTINUED

Pour the rosé, watermelon juice, and simple syrup into a large pitcher or mixing bowl, and whisk in the gelatin until dissolved. For best results, leave this in the fridge for 2 hours before freezing.

Fill your popsicle molds to the halfway mark, and return the rest of the mix to the refrigerator. Make sure the basil leaves are completely dry before you attempt this next part. Carefully float a leaf on the surface of each half-filled popsicle like, well, a lily pad. Gently place the half-filled molds in the freezer. Set the timer on your phone for 2 hours.

After catching up on a few episodes of your new favorite show or a couple of chapters of your summer read, pull the popsicles out of the freezer. Fill the rest of the way with your mix, add the popsicle sticks, and return the now-full molds to the freezer overnight. You did it! The hard part is over.

The next day, whenever you're ready to serve, remove each popsicle from the mold. Garnish with a generous pinch of Maldon sea salt—or let your guests do it.

ELEVATION NOTE: You can give these popsicles a floral, aromatic kick by swapping out the plain old simple syrup for an equal amount of home-made rose syrup. All you need to do is steep 2 oz [55 g] of dried rose petals in 2 cups [480 ml] of boiling water for 2 minutes. Strain out the petals and mix the hot rose tea with 2 cups [400 g] organic cane sugar. Let it cool, and prepare to be amazed. You can use the leftover rose syrup to flavor iced tea for the rest of your weekend. (The rose syrup will keep, covered, in the fridge for 3 to 5 days.)

AN UPGRADE FROM PICKLEBACK SHOTS AND DIRTY MARTINIS:
MANGO, PINEAPPLE, AND JALAPEÑO SHRUB

2 CUPS [480 ML] MANGO
NECTAR

2¼ CUPS [530 ML]
PINEAPPLE JUICE

6 OZ [180 ML] FRESHLY
SQUEEZED LIME JUICE
(ABOUT 6 LIMES)

4 OZ [120 ML] WHITE
VINEGAR

1 CUP [240 ML] APPLE CIDER
VINEGAR

1 CUP PLUS 2 TBSP [230 G]
ORGANIC CANE SUGAR

½ BUNCH [40 G] CHOPPED
FRESH DILL

1 LARGE JALAPEÑO, SLICED,
PLUS 12 JALAPEÑO WHEELS
(OPTIONAL) FOR GARNISH
(SEE PAGE 23)

ICE CUBES

2 OZ [60 ML] YOUR FAVORITE
CLEAR SPIRIT

12 LIME WHEELS (ABOUT
4 LIMES, OPTIONAL; SEE
PAGE 23)

Serves 12

In a traditional preparation, pieces of fruit must be strained out—but in this version, we use fruit juice to save time and effort. What makes this special is that you're pickling the entire mixture, not just one vegetable or fruit. When someone orders a shrub at Elsa or Ramona, I always caution that these aren't straightforward and sweet. It's almost like a medicinal tonic, and is slightly reminiscent of kombucha. If you're a fan of pickles, oysters, dirty martinis—really any brine-forward flavor—this is the drink for you. This particular shrub is sweet and spicy, as well as tangy.

You can mix this shrub with tequila, gin, vodka, or mezcal—which is actually my favorite—based on your preference. The recipe can be easily doubled or tripled for a party. It will keep in the fridge for weeks, and you can even drink it without a spirit, or mixed with soda water. If you're in the mood for shots, the shrub makes a much better chaser than your run-of-the-mill pickleback shot.

Add the mango nectar, pineapple juice, and lime juice to a 2-qt [2-L] glass container with a lid. (In a pinch, you can use a mixing bowl and some aluminum foil.) Add the vinegars and sugar and stir until the sugar is dissolved. Throw in the dill and jalapeños, and give everything a stir. Remember, this is similar to the process of pickling fruits or vegetables—so no need to pulverize the aromatics. Cover the mixture and store in the fridge overnight.

The next day, pour the shrub through a large, fine-mesh chinois strainer into a pitcher. It's ready to add to any tall glass filled with ice and your favorite clear spirit. You can double garnish this one with a lime wheel and jalapeño wheel nestled side by side . (The strained shrub, without the spirit, will keep, covered, in the fridge for up to 1 month.)

ELEVATION NOTE: For a smoother flavor and some flair, you can shake equal parts of the shrub and your selected spirit—2 oz [60 ml] each is a good start—with 2 dashes of orange bitters. Strain into a rocks glass filled with ice, and garnish with the lime and jalapeño wheels.

MAKE ANY NIGHT FEEL LIKE VACATION:
GINGER-CUCUMBER ROSÉ SANGRIA

ONE 750-ML BOTTLE ROSÉ

I CUP [50 G] PEELED AND THINLY SLICED FRESH GINGER

½ [200 G] SEEDLESS CUCUMBER, THINLY SLICED

5 LIME WHEELS (SEE PAGE 23)

4 OZ [120 ML] VELVET FALERNUM

ICE CUBES

4 FRESH MINT SPRIGS

Serves 4

This sangria recipe is refreshing and savory. It's pretty much the inverse of those cloying and syrupy red wine sangrias served up in restaurants that are just looking for a way to use up their leftover reds. This drink is best enjoyed on a porch with a view on a gorgeous summer night. The Velvet Falernum is a spiced Barbadian liqueur. If you have a mandolin, use it on its thinnest setting for the ginger.

Combine the rosé, ginger, cucumber, lime wheels, and Falernum in a pitcher. Give the mixture a stir, cover, and refrigerate overnight. Strain into ice-filled wineglasses, and garnish each one with a mint sprig.

YOU DON'T EVEN HAVE TO WAIT FOR THE ICE-CREAM TRUCK:
FROZEN GIN CREAMSICLE SLUSHIE

6 OZ [180 ML] ORANGE SODA

1¼ CUPS [300 ML] GIN

1 OZ [30 ML] FRESHLY SQUEEZED LEMON JUICE

1 OZ [30 ML] SIMPLE SYRUP, HOMEMADE (SEE PAGE 108)

1 OZ HEAVY CREAM, PLUS 3 CUPS [720 ML] FOR WHIPPING, OR ONE 7-OZ [200-G] CAN STORE-BOUGHT WHIPPED CREAM

½ TSP ORANGE FLOWER WATER

1 CUP [240 ML] VANILLA ICE CREAM

1 CUP [240 ML] ORANGE SHERBET

SIXTEEN 1-OZ [30-ML] ICE CUBES (OR FREEZE 2 CUPS [480 ML] WATER IN WHATEVER TRAYS YOU'VE GOT)

5 TO 6 CLEMENTINE WEDGES (SEE PAGE 22) OR LUXARDO MARASCHINO CHERRIES

5 TO 6 STRAWS

Serves 5 to 6

This decadent treat can be enjoyed on its own on a summer day, or as a boozy dessert course at a fancy dinner party. The nostalgic combination of orange and vanilla is a hit in every setting. For the orange soda, we like Blue Sky organic.

CONTINUED

Add the orange soda, gin, lemon juice, simple syrup, the 1 oz [30 ml] of heavy cream, the orange flower water, ice cream, and sherbet to your blender. Give everything a spin until combined. Add the ice and blend on high until the mixture is uniformly thick and smooth, which will take 1 to 5 minutes, depending on the power of your particular blender. If it's small, you can blend the ingredients a half—or even a third—at a time.

Now, whip that cream—use an electric mixer with a whisk attachment, and whip until soft peaks form. Or, if using store-bought, you can just pull the can out of the fridge before serving.

When you're ready to serve, pour 6 oz [180 ml] of the slushie into the bottom of a tall glass and layer ½ cup [120 ml] of the whipped cream on top. Pour another 6 oz [180 ml] of slushie over the whipped cream.

Top with a Luxardo Maraschino cherry or clementine wedge for garnish, add a straw, and enjoy.

A LITTLE SHRUB
HISTORY

Historically, shrubs served mainly as a speedy method of fruit pres-
ervation. Whenever a harvest yielded a surfeit of fruit, shrubs were a
tangy alternative to the one-note parade of jams and conserves stocked
in Colonial American households. OG shrubs combined vinegar and
chunks or slices of fruit. The fruit was eventually strained out and eaten,
while the syrup was used to flavor beverages of all sorts.

WHISKEY

...

My favorite drink is whiskey,
neat. Short and succinct,
and I like the burn.

LISA KO, AUTHOR

WHISKEY:
JUST ENJOY IT

Whiskey is an umbrella term that describes bourbon, rye, scotch, blended scotch, single malts, moonshine, and many other regional spirits. The variations are based on where and how they are produced. Many of the "rules" surrounding these spirits have changed, and are changing at this very moment, but knowing the basics can be helpful in determining your preferences. Whiskeys—including rye, bourbon, and scotch—are distilled from corn, barley, wheat, and rye, and are often mixed. To be considered bourbon, a spirit must be made with 51 percent corn, while rye whiskey is made with 51 percent rye. If you prefer a smoky flavor, try a scotch; if you'd like something smooth, and almost sweet, try bourbon; if you want something spicier and sharper, give rye a shot. You should feel free to experiment within the flavor profiles you like, and the regions you're most interested in. You'll find your own favorite in no time.

Books Are Magic

225 Smith Street
Brooklyn, NY 11231
booksaremagic.net

Books are Magic is an independent bookshop in Elsa's neighborhood, and a great resource for anything you could ever want to know (or more cocktail books).

Chef Restaurant Supplies

294-298 Bowery
New York, NY 10012
chefrestaurantsupplies.com

This store is geared more toward commercial customers, but Chef is an East Village bar and restaurant staple. You can find literally anything here.

Cherry Point

664 Manhattan Avenue
Brooklyn, NY 11222
cherrypointnyc.com

Cherry Point is another Ramona neighbor, and an absolute must for home-made charcuterie.

Cocktail Kingdom

36 West Twenty-Fifth Street, 5th Floor
New York, NY 10010
cocktailkingdom.com

Cocktail Kingdom carries the best shaker tins in the world. They provide a wide array of other barware, too. You can get lost on their website for hours.

A Cook's Companion

197 Atlantic Avenue
Brooklyn, NY 11201
acookscompanion.com

Atomizers, straws, strainers, knives—this place has it all. It's also a neighbor to Elsa.

Dual Specialty Store

91 First Avenue
New York, NY 10003
dualspecialtystorenyc.com

Dual carries the best selection of dried spices and hard-to-find ingredients that are essential components in many of our recipes.

Duke's Liquor Box

170 Franklin Street
Brooklyn, NY 11222
dukesliquorbox.com

Duke's is one of Ramona's neighbors and is another family-run business
we admire. They carry a highly curated selection of interesting spirits and
other cocktail essentials.

Eastern District

1053 Manhattan Avenue
Brooklyn, NY 11222
easterndistrictny.com

Eastern District sells a wonderful and wide variety of cheeses and other
specialty foods.

Fishs Eddy

889 Broadway
New York, NY 10003
fishseddy.com

Fishs Eddy stocks all types of glassware and ceramics, from vintage to new.
Their selection of tableware is worth checking out in person.

The Garden

921 Manhattan Avenue
Brooklyn, NY 11222
thegardenfoodmarket.com

The Garden is a family-run organic food store in Greenpoint. It's been open
for more than a decade and we love supporting their mission to provide 100
percent organic produce to the community.

Hella Bitters

22-23 Borden Avenue
Long Island City, NY 11101
hellacocktail.co

This purveyor of bitters offers an incredibly adventurous selection. You
can get everything from citrus bitters to their signature syrups online.

Homecoming

107 Franklin Street
Brooklyn, NY 11222
home-coming.com

Homecoming is a beautiful florist, home goods, and coffee shop combined.
The selection here is always tasteful and useful.

Home Studios

61 Greenpoint Avenue, Suite 225
Brooklyn, NY 11222
homestudios.nyc

Our career in hospitality would have been short-lived had it not been for this talented design team. The interiors of Elsa and Ramona are special because of Evan and Oliver Haslegrave, the founding designers. Now you can get their home accessories, furniture, and lighting via their website.

Matt White Jewelry

mattwhitejewelry.com

Matt is the incredible artist behind so many cool cocktail accessories. He's also an original member of the Elsa team.

Mouth

192 Water Street
Brooklyn, NY 11201
mouth.com

Mouth offers a wide variety of wine and spirits, as well as tons of interesting snacks and treats to enjoy along with your beverage.

The Primary Essentials

372 Atlantic Avenue
Brooklyn, NY 11217
theprimaryessentials.com

The owner of this store is a college friend with impeccable taste. If you're looking for special glassware or other beautiful home goods, this the spot to visit.

Sahadi's

187 Atlantic Avenue
Brooklyn, NY 11201
sahadis.com

Sahadi's has been selling spices, olives, dried fruit, nuts, and other specialty goods for sixty-five years. They're right across the street from Elsa, and are our go-to any time we're looking for new and interesting ingredients.

Stinky Brooklyn

215 Smith Street
Brooklyn, NY 11231
stinkybklyn.com

Stinky carries the best selection of cured meats and cheeses in Brooklyn. They've been our supplier for quality snacks from the beginning.

Two For the Pot

200 Clinton Street
Brooklyn, NY 11201

This tea shop in the Elsa neighborhood is run by the nicest people. You can get all kinds of teas and other specialty goods here for infusions and other experiments.

Whisk

231 Bedford Avenue
Brooklyn, NY 11211
Whisknyc.com

Whisk carries everything you could imagine using in your home bar.

WORD Bookstore

126 Franklin Street
Brooklyn, NY 11222
wordbookstores.com

Word is Ramona's neighborhood bookstore, with locations all over the place. They have the friendliest staff around.

Natalka Burian is the co-owner of two bars, Elsa and Ramona, as well as the author of *Welcome to the Slipstream*, a novel. She is also the cofounder of the Freya Project, a monthly fund-raising reading series that supports small nonprofit organizations in communities that do not always embrace the vital work they perform. Natalka received an MA from Columbia University, where she studied Eastern European literature, with an emphasis on the work of Leopold von Sacher-Masoch. She lives in Brooklyn with her husband and two daughters.

Scott Schneider is the co-owner of Elsa and Ramona. Born in upstate New York, he moved to Brooklyn in 2004 to study design at Pratt Institute. Starting as a barback with zero experience the night the original Elsa opened in 2007, he quickly discovered his passion for crafting cocktails with an emphasis on house-made ingredients. Within a year he started managing Elsa, and in 2013, he opened Ramona with his brother, Jay, and sister-in-law, Natalka. Four years later, Elsa reopened with the same team, and Scott continues to oversee the cocktail program at both bars. He currently lives in Greenpoint, Brooklyn, and has been interviewed by the *New Yorker*, the *New York Times*, *New York Magazine*, and *Interview Magazine*, among others.

ACKNOWLEDGMENTS

We owe a tremendous amount of gratitude to Zeb Millett, Jeremy Wilson, and Marcos Toledo, as well as all of our invaluable colleagues at Elsa and Ramona, past and present. Special thanks to Brandon Davey and Matt White, who have endured all of the small-business growing pains with us.

Thanks to our brilliant editor Camaren Subhiyah who helped us craft this book and worked nights and holidays to make it happen, Vanessa Dina for the perfect design, Tera Killip for all the research and ace production advice, Zaneta Jung for keeping us on track, Christine Carswell for championing the project, and Deborah Kops and Marie Oishi for the eagle eye. Thanks to the entire team at Chronicle who support us in so many ways. Our appreciation is endless for Kate Johnson, who is the very best, and everyone at Wolf Literary. Extra-special thanks to the brilliant Jordan Awan and Morgan Elliott.

We are deeply grateful to the incredibly talented Alice Gao, Pierce Harrison, Rebecca Bartoshesky, and Jocelyn Cabral. Thanks to all of our amazing contributors—Lauren Duca, Jessica Valenti, Lisa Ko, Violette, Morgan Jerkins, Emma Straub, Lauren Elkin, Jami Attenberg, Eleanore Pienta, Sunita Mani, and Lenora Lapidus.

This book would not have been possible without the support of our dear friends with great taste, Yelena Mokritsky, Dominic Espinosa, Garret Smith, Dave Gooblar, Ben Epstein, Amanda Simon, Nonie Brzyski, Dan Wagner, Ben Duarte, and the Preview Wear team, Henry Northington, Collin Lewis, Alfie Palao, Kevin Showkat, Mike Sweeney, Elizabeth and Michelle Dilk, Alex Goldstein, Nick Roechley, Daniella Urdinlaiz, Andrew Kay, and Kaitlyn Pepe. Thanks to Evan and Oliver Haslegrave, and the entire Home team.

Thanks to our supportive families, Nancy and Arnold Schneider, Irka Zazulak, Elisabeth Schneider, and Olesh and Milya Burian.

This book, and our lives, would not be the same without Eva Hogan and Jay Schneider. And always, thanks to Viola and Leo for being constant sources of inspiration.

INDEX

A few years ago I would have said that my favorite drink was a Manhattan or a dry martini—not because those were actually my favorites, but because I cared more then about what people thought. I don't give a shit anymore: I love piña coladas. They taste amazing, they're fun, and I was drinking one when I had my first date with my husband.

JESSICA VALENTI, AUTHOR